HOLLYWOOD'S PRE-CODE HORRORS 1931–1934

by Raymond Valinoti, Jr.

HOLLYWOOD'S PRE-CODE HORRORS 1931–1934
By Raymond Valinoti, Jr.
© 2016, ALL RIGHTS RESERVED
No part of this book may be reproduced in any form or by any means, electronic, mechanical, digital, photocopying, or recording, except for inclusion of a review, without permission in writing from the publisher or Author.

Published in the USA by:
BearManor Media
P O Box 71426
Albany, Georgia 31708
www.bearmanormedia.com

ISBN: 978-1-62933-086-0
BearManor Media, Albany, Georgia
Printed in the United States of America
Book design by Robbie Adkins, www.adkinsconsult.com

TABLE OF CONTENTS

Introduction v
Dracula. 1
Frankenstein. 11
Dr. Jekyll and Mr. Hyde 19
Murders in the Rue Morgue 31
Freaks. 39
White Zombie. 47
Doctor X 55
The Most Dangerous Game. 63
The Old Dark House 71
Photos 78
The Mask of Fu Manchu 85
The Mummy 93
The Island of Lost Souls 99
The Vampire Bat 107
Mystery of the Wax Museum 113
King Kong 121
Murders in the Zoo 127
Supernatural. 135
The Invisible Man 141
The Black Cat. 149
Afterword. 157
Bibliography. 162
Index 166

HOLLYWOOD'S PRE-CODE HORRORS

INTRODUCTION

On March 31, 1930, the Motion Pictures Producers and Distributors of America (MPPDA) formally swore to adhere to the newly established Production Code. The MPPDA had been established in December 1921, in the wake of scandals that threatened the motion picture industry's public standing. The purpose of the MPPDA was to carefully monitor upcoming films to ensure that they were morally acceptable to the public. The MPPDA thus prevented the U.S. government from policing the films. In order to mollify the government, the organization appointed U.S. Postmaster General Will Hays as its head.

With the conversion of motion pictures from silents to talkies in the late 1920s, the MPPDA fretted about potentially-offensive dialogue. The Production Code intended to strengthen a 1927 edict on "taboo" subjects including nudity, drug abuse, and sexual perversion. But for the next four years, the Code did not rigidly enforce its guidelines, despite protests from the Legion of Decency and other religious groups. Finally on July 1, 1934, the MPPDA caved in and invigorated the Production Code.

Before that, Hollywood created outrageous films brimming with salaciousness and brutality. Even the cartoons pushed the boundaries of propriety, particularly Max Fleischer's Betty Boop cartoons. In defying the Code, the film producers were simply catering to American box office patrons. *Some* filmgoers were straitlaced, particularly in the Bible Belt, but others, especially in the big cities, were not easily shocked. They savored the raciness provided by novels and stage shows; they expected films to provide the same. Since the Great Depression plagued the movie business, the producers were desperate to keep afloat. If violent and sexy films remained profitable, they would continue to make them.

It was in this relatively-permissible environment that the American horror genre originated. Horror films did not immediately spring up and flood the cinemas. Universal bought the rights to the successful Broadway play *Dracula,* based on Bram Stoker's vampire novel. If the film did poorly at the box office, the studio would not have bothered making other horror films. But it not only was a hit, but it made a new star out of Bela Lugosi, the Hungarian actor, in the title role. The studio hoped lightning would strike again with another chiller, *Frankenstein.* This adaptation of Mary Shelley's man-made monster saga made *more* money than *Dracula* and created another star, English thespian Boris Karloff, who played the monster. The verdict was in—the public enjoyed being frightened.

In the following years before the Code was enforced, Universal produced more chillers and launched another actor to stardom, Claude Rains. Paramount, Metro-Goldwyn-Mayer (MGM), United Artists, Warner Brothers, and RKO jumped on the horror bandwagon. Even Majestic, a minor, low-budget studio, produced a horror film. Lugosi and Karloff capitalized on their new macabre personas in some of these films. The distinguished English stage actor Lionel Atwill became typecast as a bogeyman, and screen beauty Fay Wray became typecast as a scream queen. Even actors who never were pigeonholed in chillers made vivid impressions in the chillers they *did* appear in, like Fredric March and Charles Laughton. The films were also important stepping stones for rising stars like Myrna Loy and Carole Lombard. (Although both actresses were unhappy with these assignments.)

How did filmmakers utilize these films' grisly potential? Certainly the films' premises *seemed* grisly. Not only did they focus on imaginary creatures like resurrected mummies and scientific fabrications like invisible maniacs, they also explored warped behavior like necrophilia and sexual sadism. In truth, some movies *did* exploit the bloodcurdling concepts to the hilt. In fact, MGM's *Freaks* and Paramount's *Murders in the Zoo* went too far, tarnishing their box office prospects. Other movies handled the shocks delicately. Universal's filmmakers tended to restrain the shocks, either out of concern of negative feedback (as was the case of its first horror film *Dracula*) or to deliver the chills with subtlety (as was the case of *The Mummy*). Not surprisingly, the tamer shockers provoked less controversy than the wilder ones.

The filmmakers didn't only take advantage of the lax Production Code to indulge in sex and violence. They also provided sharp social commentaries. For instance, *Murders in the Rue Morgue* and *The Old Dark House* took satirical stabs at religion. *The Most Dangerous Game,* unlike its literary source, denounced the sport of hunting. The films touched on unpleasant realities like drug addiction and police brutality. Many of them alluded to the Great Depression. In *King Kong,* Ann Darrow (Fay Wray) accepts an offer to participate in a risky film project on an uncharted island because she is penniless and starving. Jack Griffin (Claude Rains) creates a formula that makes him *The Invisible Man,* hoping his scientific innovation will be his escape route out of poverty. Not all of the social commentaries were enlightening and constructive. *The Mask of Fu Manchu* explicitly pandered to White Americans' anti-Oriental prejudices. It didn't so much indoctrinate this bigotry as it reflected it. This was an undeniable if reprehensible aspect of Depression-era society.

While the filmmakers supplied their horrors with jolts and insight, they tried to provide them with likable and relatable characters. Comic relief figures often appeared in them to provide box office patrons a respite. Occasionally the hero or heroine who challenged the fiend was humorous, like Lee Tracy as a wisecracking reporter in *Doctor X* and Glenda Farrell in a distaff version of the role in *Mystery of the Wax Museum.* Even the funny characters were given outrageous material in these pre-Code horrors, consisting of suggestive jokes. These films also had sweet romantic duos who would live happily ever after the villain was vanquished. In such films as *Dracula, White Zombie,* and *The Mummy,* the villain would threaten to take the heroine away from her lover.

Occasionally when the scenarists adapted literary properties to the screen, they even softened the monsters. Robert Louis Stevenson's egoistic Dr. Jekyll became an idealistic if misguided scientist in Rouben Mamoulian's film version. H.G. Wells' invisible chemist Griffin, who was unfeeling and unscrupulous even before he dematerialized, became a kind person whose invisibility formula made him criminally insane in James Whale's film version. They were also given romantic interests who recognized their fundamental goodness and grieved for them when they went astray.

The pre-Code horrors released between 1931 and 1934 were a varied lot, not only in aesthetic quality, but in audience reactions. Some films like *King Kong* and *The Invisible Man* were big hits, while others like *Freaks* and *The Island of Lost Souls* lost money. This book devotes each chapter to one of them, from *Dracula* (1931) to *The Black Cat* (1934). The author intends to examine each film in the context of the period it was made. Issues with censors during production and after release will be discussed. Contemporary critical and audience reactions will also be cited. The author will also explain how each film reflects the times when they were made. This work makes no pretense in being the definite authority on pre-Code horror film history, but it tries to inform the readers how the laxly-enforced Production Code shaped these chillers, most which are considered classics today. The author also hopes to entertain the readers with anecdotes and critiques, perhaps encouraging them to see them for the first time or to see them again.

King Kong's sequel, *Son of Kong*, released the same year as the original, has been excluded from this book. Although the follow-up has horrific elements, it is not a full-fledged horror film. The titular creature isn't *supposed* to be frightening, just comical and lovable. Regrettably, one full-fledged pre-Code horror is unavailable for reappraisal. The original English-language version of RKO's *The Monkey's Paw* (1933), based on W.W. Jacobs's macabre tale, is still missing. A French-dubbed version is supposed to exist, but even if it was accessible to the public, the author could not fully evaluate the film's merits on the basis of this print. Hollywood's pre-Code horrors should not only be judged by their visual qualities but by their dialogue as well. As previously noted, these films provided naughty innuendo. The actors would also deliver their lines suggestively, particularly Lionel Atwill. His salacious thesping cannot be fully appreciated in any "foreign" language version dubbed by any other actor. *The Old Dark House* and *Mystery of the Wax Museum* were once considered lost, but now original prints are available to the public. Hopefully, an original print of *The Monkey's Paw* will be unearthed in the future. Considering the fact that 1930s films were composed of the highly flammable nitrate, we should be grateful that all of Hollywood's other pre-Code horrors remain intact.

Raymond Valinoti, Jr.

x

HOLLYWOOD'S PRE-CODE HORRORS

DRACULA (1931)

Released February 12, 1931; A Universal Picture; *Director:* **Tod Browning;** *Producer:* **Carl Laemmle, Jr.;** *Associate Producer:* **E.M. Asher;** *Screenplay:* **Garrett Fort,** *based on Bram Stoker's novel and Hamilton Deane and John L. Balderston's play; Scenario Supervisor:* **Charles A. Logue;** *Director of Photography:* **Karl Freund;** *Art Director:* **Charles B. Hall;** *Editor:* **Milton Carruth;** *Supervising Editor:* **Maurice Pivar;** *Photographic Effects:* **Frank J. Booth;** *Music Conductor:* **Heinz Roemheld;** *Makeup:* **Jack P. Pierce; 75 minutes.**

Cast: **Bela Lugosi (Dracula), Helen Chandler (Mina Seward), David Manners (Jonathan Harker), Dwight Frye (Renfield), Edward Van Sloan (Professor Van Helsing), Herbert Bunston (Dr. Seward), Frances Dade (Lucy Weston), Joan Standing (The Maid), Charles Gerrard (Martin), Moon Carroll (Briggs), Josephine Velez (Grace), Michael Visaroff (Innkeeper), Carla Laemmle, Nicholas Bela, Donald Murphy (Coach Passengers), Tod Browning (Harbor Master).**

SYNOPSIS: *British businessman Renfield leaves England for Transylvania to arrange a lease of the Carfax Abbey in England for the nobleman Count Dracula. But the Count, a centuries-old vampire, attacks Renfield and makes him a slave who sustains himself on the blood of small animals. With Renfield in tow, Dracula sails for England, where nobody knows he's a vampire. Once the Count is there, he immediately starts attacking London's inhabitants. Meanwhile, British authorities find the obviously-insane Renfield and commit him to a sanitarium run by one Dr. Seward. Dracula is attracted to Seward's daughter, Mina, and starts drinking her blood to turn her into a vampire. The Dutch vampire expert Professor Van Helsing arrives in England to foil the Count's scheme. After a battle of wits between Van Helsing and Dracula, the professor destroys the vampire by putting a stake in his heart. Mina is freed from the Count's spell and is reunited with her fiancé, Jonathan Harker.*

When the British studio Hammer released its splashy version of Bram Stoker's novel in 1958, the film's blunt goriness and sensuality made Universal's 1931 version seem tame. Today, the average filmgoer, accustomed to far bloodier and raunchier horrors, wouldn't find the 1931 version the least bit shocking. Of all the pre-Code chillers examined in this book, this film is the mildest. How could this relatively-innocuous work initiate the horror genre in Hollywood?

To understand *Dracula*'s huge impact on American filmgoers when it was first released, one should look at the movie industry in the early 1930s. Throughout the silent and early talkie eras, very few films were true horrors. There were spooky elements in a lot of mysteries, but these alleged ghosts and demons were explained away as the crafty ruses of mere mortals. Some grotesque creatures, particularly those played by Lon Chaney, the Man of a Thousand Faces, capered across the screen. But few of them were supernatural creatures or human-made monstrosities; they were ordinary people who looked extraordinarily ugly, like Quasimodo in *The Hunchback of Notre Dame* (1923), or else they masqueraded as otherworldly creatures, like the detective hero disguised as a vampire in *London After Midnight* (1927). There were several adaptations of Robert Louis Stevenson's *The Strange Case of Dr. Jekyll and Mr. Hyde*. But as frightening as Mr. Hyde could be, particularly as portrayed by John Barrymore in Paramount's 1920 version, he was just the outward manifestation of Dr. Jekyll's dark side, not an otherworldly or artificial being.

Universal may have never brought *Dracula* to the screen had it not been a Broadway hit in the 1920s. Carl Laemmle, Sr., the venerable head of Universal, initially objected to purchasing the rights to the vampire story. He recoiled at the idea of producing a film about a supernatural, bloodsucking fiend. But another studio, Metro-Goldwyn-Mayer, which had profited from a glut of Lon Chaney shockers directed by Tod Browning, considered acquiring the property for their star. Repulsed as Laemmle was with *Dracula's* theme, he saw its box office potential. He didn't want any rival studio to profit from the vampire story. With the enthusiastic support of his son Carl, Jr., Universal's General Manager, he secured a deal with Stoker's widow and the play's authors. Tod Browning was hired as director. Chaney, having starred in the studio's *The Hunchback of Notre Dame* and *The Phantom of the Opera*, was expected to play the title role.

On August 26, 1930, the Man of a Thousand Faces died of bronchial cancer. After Universal considered a few actors for the starring role, they finally settled on Bela Lugosi, who had played the part on Broadway and on a cross-country tour. The studio fretted over whether or not the Production Code would approve of a story of an honest-to-goodness monster. Universal was determined to placate the censors, assuring them that *Dracula* was a "tale of horror and mystery, with love theme for relief." After examining copies of the book and play, the Production Code head Jason S. Joy gave the studio his approval. The Code did not forbid films about genuine supernatural creatures like vampires. There was no controversy about them because Hollywood hadn't yet made any such films.

Although the Production Code gave Universal the green light, the studio tinkered with the play's spicy elements. On stage, Dracula passionately kissed his potential female victim on the lips; in the film, he daintily kisses her hand. The studio felt that unsophisticated cinemagoers would find a bloodsucking vampire sufficiently overwhelming; an overtly amorous one would be too much. Carl, Jr. objected to the screenplay's depiction of Dracula's attack on Renfield: "Dracula should go only for women and not men." This segment was filmed anyway.

When *Dracula* was released, Universal's publicity department would exploit the vampire's sex appeal. Its sales line was "The Strangest Passion the World Has Ever Known." Advertisements across the country played up the vampire's allure for women. A poster at the Strand Theatre in Louisville depicted Bela Lugosi hovering over Frances Dade (playing Lucy, a lovely victim) with the proclamation "Beware of the Kiss of Dracula—the Caress that Burns like a Flame of Fire!" Another *Dracula* ad at the Capitol

Theatre in Atlanta, Georgia, was a cartoon of a voluptuous woman staring up at Lugosi's image above the title, "as if worshipping the God of Sex," as horror scholar Gregory William Mank has written.

Lugosi had already titillated female spectators as the Count on stage. In an interview with *Motion Picture Magazine,* published in January 1931, a month before the film's release, Bela explained:

"When I was playing Dracula on the stage, my audiences were women. Women. There were men, too. Escorts the women had brought with them. For reasons only their dark subconscious knew. In order to establish a subtle sex intimacy. Contact. In order to cling to and feel the sensuous thrill of protection. Men did not come of their own volition. Women did. Came—and knew an ecstasy dragged from the depths of unspeakable things. Came—and then came back again. And again.

"Women wrote me letters. Ah, what letters women wrote me. Young girls. Women from seventeen to thirty. Letters of a horrible hunger. Asking me if I cared only for a maiden's blood. Asking me if I had done the play because I was in reality that sort of Thing. And through these letters, couched in terms of shuddering, transparent fear, there ran the hideous note of—hope. They hoped that I was Dracula. They hoped that my love was the love of—*Dracula.*"

An adolescent girl in Johnstown, Pennsylvania named Hope Lininger was particularly infatuated with Lugosi's image on screen. For years, she wrote fan letters to Lugosi. It is said that she came to Hollywood in the 1940s to be near her idol. A decade later, she married Bela and remained his wife until his death on August 16, 1956.

Lugosi's suave Count, with his slicked-back black hair and his clean-shaven Byronic looks, was quite a contrast to the vampire in Bram Stoker's novel, an elderly white-haired man with a bushy mustache and hairy hands. Stoker's Dracula does become younger when he drinks his victims' blood, but he never becomes handsome. Had both the Broadway play and the Universal film depicted the Count as he is in the book, neither would have been a box office hit. Lugosi's image of Dracula did more than ensure their success; it has superseded Stoker's image in the popular imagination.

Most of the film lacks the ads' salaciousness. An exception is Dracula's attack on Renfield. Lugosi's ravenous expression as he approaches Renfield (Dwight Frye) enhances the scene's suggestiveness. Director Tod Browning, with the assistance of cinematographer Karl Freund, imbues the film with an appropriate macabre aura, particularly in the opening scenes in Transylvania. But as countless horror scholars and fans have noted, most of the movie's shocks—the bloodsucker killing the crew of the ship he takes to London, Mina's vampirized friend Lucy preying on children, Dracula offering Renfield a horde of rats if he will do the vampire's bidding—are *described*, rather than depicted. Browning and Freund effectively utilize *Dracula*'s cinematic potential in the Transylvania setting, but once the Count leaves home, the film, with a few exceptions, reverts to a filmed play. Van Helsing's staking of Dracula occurs off-screen with only the Count's cries to indicate his destruction. (These cries were removed from the soundtrack when *Dracula* was reissued in 1938, but they are now restored in present prints and on commercial home video.)

Even a suggestive scene, where Mina, under Dracula's spell, tries to vampirize her unwitting fiancé Jonathan Harker (David Manners) before Van Helsing (Edward Van Sloan) intervenes, is handled tamely. Helen Chandler as Mina is attractively but demurely dressed. Although she stares longingly at Harker, Chandler makes no seductive gestures, nor does she have such lines. In another scene, Renfield leers at Seward's maid (Joan Standing), causing her to faint. The lunatic menacingly approaches her. Suddenly, the scene ends. The maid reappears in the film, apparently unscathed. The abruptly-truncated earlier scene was intended to tease the filmgoers. It was supposed to end with the lunatic snatching a fly from her clothing. But this payoff was cut before *Dracula* was released.

The play *Dracula* enticed theatergoers with the slogan "The Ultimate in Horror." But film audiences were less sophisticated and worldly than stage audiences. When Universal first released *Dracula*, promoters tried to assure the public that it wasn't offensive. One advertisement proclaimed, "Dracula will haunt you ... he will thrill ... and yet amuse." This tagline's message was obvious—*Dracula* may have been a scary film, but it was harmless entertainment. To further assuage box office patrons' misgivings, the publicists kidded the film's spookiness. New Yorkers could see placards at the Roxy

Theatre with goofy statements like "I'll be on your neck" and "Good to the last gasp!" Comical promotional stunts were also employed. For instance, paperhangers in formal dress and Dracula masks installed a *Dracula* twenty-sheet billboard on Hollywood Boulevard.

Determined to entice people to see the film, the publicity department tried not to overemphasize its macabre premise. The editors of Fox West Coast Theatre's newsletter advised promoters, "It would not be very good policy to use coffins . . . in other words . . . don't go too far in gruesome exploitation . . . keep it weird . . . but don't suggest dead bodies." The same newsletter warned them, "This is hardly classed as a child's picture. We would not attempt any contest among school children . . . it is a bit too nightmarish." *Dracula*'s advertisements would only target mature box office patrons.

Universal was more worried about American filmgoers than it was about filmgoers in other countries. Censorship restrictions were looser outside the United States. A Spanish language version for the "foreign" market, in the period before dubbing techniques were perfected, was filmed at the same time as the English language version. The Spanish language crew, under the direction of George Melford, exploits *Dracula*'s cinematic potential more fully than Tod Browning's English language crew. For instance, Browning's version doesn't depict Dracula terrorizing the crew on his trip to London. But Melford's version crosscuts between the vampire's menacing emergence from his coffin and the crewmen's terrified reactions. Granted, the horror in this segment is restrained, but it is actually *shown*, not *told*.

Melford's department is also more daring in handling *Dracula*'s sensual elements. The heroine's attempt to seduce her fiancé is far more brazen in the Spanish language version than in the English language version. Her attire is more revealing and her physical actions are more demonstrative. Lupita Tovar's lustful behavior in the scene makes Helen Chandler's actions chaste by comparison.

If Tod Browning was worried that his English language production would offend patrons, it was uncharacteristic. His previous collaborations with Lon Chaney at MGM had macabre themes. For instance, in *The Unknown* (1927), Chaney plays a circus performer who has his arms amputated because the woman he adores cannot stand being embraced. In *West of Zanzibar* (1928), Chaney forces a young girl to become a prostitute because he believes she is the daughter of the fiend who tried to kill him. Browning eagerly exploited these films' creepy themes, and audiences relished them. A year after *Dracula* came out, the director would pull out all the stops in delivering the grisliness in MGM's *Freaks*, and it was too much for filmgoers, resulting in a box office fiasco. (More about *Freaks* later.)

Browning's tepid handling of *Dracula*'s scenario may not have only been due to the studio's wariness. According to David Manners, who played Jonathan Harker, Karl Freund did most of the actual directing, while Tod just hung around "back in the shadows." Carla Laemmle, the senior Laemmle's niece, who appeared in the opening scene in a coach in Transylvania, recalled that Browning was absent from this shooting. George Melford knew no Spanish and needed an interpreter to handle his *Dracula* production, but he benefited from the enthusiastic and skillful guidance of producer Paul Kohner.

Browning does not deserve all the blame for the English language version's missed opportunities. After three weeks of shooting, Universal ordered the director to hurry up and finish. The studio was having financial difficulties due to the Depression. Lugosi later recalled that the studio was "hell-bent on saving money—they even cut rubber erasers in half—everything that Tod Browning wanted to do was queried. Couldn't it be done cheaper? Wouldn't it be just as effective if. . . .? That sort of thing. It was most dispiriting." This also explains why after the first few reels, *Dracula* becomes for the most part a static talkfest.

When Universal viewed the completed rough cut, the studio insisted it should be tightened and re-edited. Laemmle, Jr. believed that Browning had made too many master shots and not enough cutaways. But in the process of trimming the film for release, Universal marred its continuity. Renfield's menacing of the maid is abruptly curtailed. There's also a jump cut in the Transylvanian castle sequence where Dracula's wives threaten Renfield before the Count stops them. Browning was bitter at Universal for inadvertently hampering his film and for not allowing him to help edit it;

he still complained about this when he saw *Dracula* on television in the late 1950s.

Despite these liabilities, *Dracula* was an enormous box office success. Press accounts reported that over fifty thousand people paid to see the film at New York City's Roxy Theater during its first two days of screenings. Even the film critics liked the film. They may have liked it because it pulled its punches on scares. Tom Weaver, Michael Brunas and John Brunas observe in their book *Universal Horrors* that "... most critical comments suggest that even a slightly stronger presentation would have proved completely unacceptable to the genteel audiences of the time." *Variety*'s review opined, "Such a treatment called for the utmost delicacy of handling because the thing is so completely ultra-sensational on its serious side, and the faintest excess of telling would make it grotesque." One critic found *Dracula* a little too strong for his liking. Philip K. Scheuer wrote in the *Los Angeles Times,* "Where the cinema transcription falls short, it seems to me, is in its insistence of being too real, overly explicit . . . [It]s manner of storytelling is that of the stage, with imagination largely sacrificed to theatricality."

Although a flood of filmgoers paid to see *Dracula,* not everybody enjoyed it. Some patrons fainted, and this troubled Jason S. Joy: "Is this the beginning of a cycle which ought to be retarded or killed?" A lot of people complained about the film to the MPPDA, which was responsible for the Production Code. One viewer called the film "the most horrible thing. The author must have had a distorted mind and I cannot understand why it was produced. I cannot speak too strongly against this picture for children." Parent-Teacher Association (PTA) Report Chairman Marjorie Ross Davis informed the MPPDA she only saw the first fifteen minutes of *Dracula* but "felt I could stand no more ... It should be withdrawn from public showing, as children, [the] weak-minded and all classes attend motion pictures indiscriminately."

One particular comment foreshadowed the massive and powerful crusades to clean up films that not only resulted in the strengthening of the Code but the temporary ban of horror films as well: "This picture should be protested by every previewing organization. Its insane horrible details shown to millions of impressionable children, to adults already bowed down by human misery, will do an infinite amount of harm." Universal's qualms about American filmgoers' sensitivities were justified to a certain degree. But the condemnations couldn't jeopardize *Dracula*'s popularity. The studio knew that Americans enjoyed being frightened. Carl Laemmle, Sr. himself put aside his initial misgivings to boast of *Dracula*'s success: "The People are simply eating it up ... I knew it was good but I didn't know it was that good, even after I had seen it in the projection room." So Universal immediately planned another chiller. The studio hoped to capitalize on Bela Lugosi's new stardom. Instead, it would establish a brand new star.

FRANKENSTEIN (1931)

Released November 21, 1931; A Universal Picture; *Director:* **James Whale**; *Producer:* **Carl Laemmle, Jr.**; *Screenplay:* **Garrett Fort, Francis Edward Farogh, John Russell, and Robert Florey**; *Adaptation:* **John L. Balderston**; *Based on the novel by Mary Shelley and the play by Peggy Webling; Associate Producer:* **E.M. Asher**; *Scenario Editor:* **Richard L. Schayer**; *Continuity:* **Tom Reed**; *Photography:* **Arthur Edeson**; *Supervising Editor:* **Maurice Pivar**; *Editor:* **Clarence Kolster**; *Art Directors:* **Charles D. Hall and Herman Rosse**; *Makeup:* **Jack P. Pierce**; *Special Electrical Effects:* **Kenneth Strickfaden, Frank Graves, and Raymond Lindsay**; *Music Director:* **David Broekman**; *Music:* **Bernhard Kaun**; 71 minutes.

Cast: **Colin Clive (Henry Frankenstein), Mae Clarke (Elizabeth), John Boles (Victor Moritz), Boris Karloff (The Monster), Edward Van Sloan (Dr. Waldman), Frederick Kerr (Baron Frankenstein), Dwight Frye (Fritz), Lionel Belmore (Burgomaster), Marilyn Harris (Maria), Michael Mark (Ludwig).**

SYNOPSIS: Young scientist Henry Frankenstein and his addled, hunchbacked assistant Fritz steal parts of corpses in a cemetery to create a synthetic being. Frankenstein orders Fritz to steal a brain from a medical college. When Fritz accidentally destroys a normal brain there, he grabs and runs off with an abnormal brain. Unaware of this, Frankenstein inserts the brain into the man-made creature. He brings the creature to life via electricity on a stormy night in a watchtower. At first, Frankenstein is delighted with his creation, but he's upset when the creature, agitated by Fritz's torch, becomes violent. When the monster, provoked by Fritz, kills his tormentor, the young scientist suffers a nervous breakdown. Frankenstein's mentor Dr. Waldman vows to destroy the monster while Frankenstein recuperates with his fiancée Elizabeth at home. But when Waldman plans to dissect him, the monster strangles him to death. Fleeing from the watchtower, the monster meets and befriends a little girl named Maria. He accidentally drowns her in the lake and runs away bewildered and distressed. Meanwhile, Frankenstein plans to marry Elizabeth, but his friend Victor Moritz tells him Waldman's corpse has been found and the monster has disappeared. After the monster terrorizes Elizabeth, Frankenstein vows to hunt him down and destroy him. Maria's grieving father Ludwig, the Burgomaster, and the other villagers in Frankenstein's hometown of Goldstadt join the scientist. Frankenstein and the monster confront and fight each other in a windmill. After the monster throws his creator out of a window in the mill, the villagers set the place on fire. The monster perishes in the flames, but Frankenstein recovers from his fall.

Frankenstein would make even more money for Universal than *Dracula*. But the film might not have been so popular if the studio went ahead with Robert Florey and Garrett Fort's original script. This scenario is far more grisly than the released film's revised screenplay. Henry Frankenstein is a paranoid monomaniac who abuses the monster with a whip and a hot poker and eventually goes completely mad, "reeling around the room, alternately laughing and crying, careening against whatever appears in his way." The monster is a malevolent brute devoid of any sensitivity; his eyes "gleam with animal cunning." Maria's aggrieved father fatally shoots both scientist and monster.

Florey wanted Bela Lugosi to play Frankenstein. (Lugosi's performance as Dr. Mirakle in the Florey-directed *Murders in the Rue Morgue* gives a strong indication how the Hungarian actor would have portrayed him.) Universal, however, wanted Lugosi to play the monster. Bela was unhappy with the nonspeaking role of the monster. "Anyone can moan and grunt," he bemoaned. When Universal hired the Englishman James Whale to direct *Frankenstein*, Lugosi was dropped from the picture. Whale's friend Gavin Lambert later explained, "He talked about the fact that Lugosi was basically scary and scared audiences, and he said the monster, in his view—although he could scare people—was also scared."

In later films, Lugosi believably brought pathos to his horror roles. As the Sayer of the Law in *The Island of Lost Souls,* raging at his heartless creator Dr. Moreau, he is as heartbreaking as he is horrific. He also elicits sympathy as the tormented Dr. Witus Werdegast in *The Black Cat.* But when *Frankenstein* was ready to be filmed, Bela's only horror role had been as Dracula, a sinister fiend who deserved to be destroyed.

Under Whale's supervision, Francis Edwards Faragoh provided a rewrite which softened the creature's personality. The monster was still dangerous, but he was also childlike and vulnerable. All of his killings were either provoked or accidental. Although the revised version suggested the monster was sexually attracted to women, he was never guilty of rape, as implied in Florey's original draft. Unlike the monster in Shelley's novel, this one was inarticulate. But like his literary counterpart, he was a sympathetic character who was driven to violence by society's rejection. The MPPDA accepted the final script, with reservations. They were concerned about certain aspects, "those gruesome ones that will certainly bring an audience reaction of horror." These gruesome aspects were the body of a hanged man in the opening graveyard scene and the monster's murder of Dr. Frankenstein's assistant Fritz (Dwight Frye).

The English actor Boris Karloff, who had been working in films for more than a decade, was the perfect choice for the monster, frightening yet pitiful. He agreed with the director that the creature should be depicted this way:

"Whale and I both saw the character as an innocent one. Within the heavy restrictions of my makeup, I tried to play it that way. This was a pathetic creature who, like us all, had neither wish nor say in his creation, and certainly did not wish upon itself the hideous image which automatically terrified humans it tried to befriend. The most heart-rending aspect of the creature's life, for us, was his ultimate desertion by his creator. It was though man, in his blundering, searching attempts to improve himself, was to find himself deserted by God."

Universal's makeup master Jack Pierce meticulously created Karloff's now iconic square-headed countenance. The first version featured forehead clamps and a deformed lower lip. The monster's appearance was softened for the film, making him look less hideous. James Whale probably insisted on the modification, making it easier for filmgoers to feel sorry for him. Nevertheless, a lot of people on the set were unnerved by Karloff's makeup. Boris's character was supposed to terrify Mae Clarke's character in one scene. The leading lady asked Karloff to signal up-camera when approaching her. He complied by wiggling his finger so she could see it. Clarke later recalled, "Between Karloff's perfect performance and my throwing myself so thoroughly into the role, I feared I would drop dead."

Seven-year-old Marilyn Harris's character Maria wasn't supposed to be scared by the monster. In fact, the young actress wasn't. The English actor treated her with great kindness. She performed with Karloff on location at Sherwood Lake, a privately-owned body of water in the Santa Monica mountains. A caravan of cars and trucks traveled to the area for two days' shooting. Harris remembered, "Boris Karloff was in his makeup and nobody wanted to ride with him, but he didn't bother me. I had such love for that man. I went over to him and said, 'May I please ride with you?' and he said I could."

It was a difficult on location shoot. Maria and the monster were supposed to toss flowers into the lake and see them float. The monster would then put Maria into the water, thinking she would also float. To his alarm, Maria would sink to the bottom. Karloff wanted to gently ease the girl in the water. Whale insisted that the actor toss her in. They argued about it for a while, but Whale got his way.

The first take backfired; Marilyn remained afloat because her costume billowed with air. The girl's back was hurt from hitting the water, and she didn't want to do another take. But she had no say in the matter. At that time, before child labor legislation was strengthened, the studios were not obliged to ensure the children's safety. Whale assured her, "If you do it again, I'll give you anything you want." Marilyn asked Karloff not to throw her in the water so roughly on the second take. Boris was sympathetic, but he told her he had to hurl her into the water. Luckily for Marilyn, the second take went smoothly.

People in rowboats out of camera range fished Marilyn out. "I had had swimming lessons, but I never really practiced swimming underwater," she later said. "When he threw me in again, I managed to stay under and swim out of camera range, but that wasn't skill. I did it out of fear." Whale kept his promise; Marilyn asked for a dozen hard-boiled eggs. The director gave her *two* dozen eggs.

Frankenstein's final screenplay also mitigated Henry Frankenstein's character. Gone was the physical abuse; in the film, Fritz torments the creature. James Whale envisioned the scientist as "normally and extremely intelligent, a sane and lovable person, never unsympathetic, even to the monster." The director believed Colin Clive "had exactly the right kind of tenacity to go through with anything, together with the kind of romantic quality which makes strong men leave civilization to shoot big game." He also felt the actor could convey "levelheadedness," even "in his craziest moments."

In the movie, Clive fulfills Whale's vision. His Henry Frankenstein is a sensitive if misguided soul. He can be hysterical, particularly when he sees his creation come to life, but he never loses his humanity. And when the monster kills people, the scientist risks his own life to stop him. "I made him with these hands, and with these hands I will destroy him," the doctor declares. Frankenstein doesn't acknowledge his irresponsible abandonment of the creature, but he feels responsible for the victims.

Despite Whale's softening of the scientist and the monster, Universal's sales staff were worried about *Frankenstein*'s box office appeal. They believed Carl Laemmle, Jr. was out of his mind for pursuing this project. W.R. Wilkerson, who was on the *Frankenstein* set, wrote in *The Hollywood Reporter*, "They reasoned that *Dracula* was a hit because it was a new screen idea, and that *Frankenstein* was a repeat, but more horrible as a shocker."

Carl Laemmle, Sr. also had qualms about *Frankenstein*. "I didn't believe in that production," he later admitted. "I said to Junior, 'I don't believe in horror pictures. It's morbid . . . People don't want that sort of thing.' Only Junior wanted it. Only Junior stood out for it and he said to me, 'Yes they do, Pop. They do want that sort of thing. Just give me a chance and I'll show you.'"

Boris Karloff himself wasn't sure. After seeing the completed film, he told fellow cast member Edward Van Sloan he feared it would "ruin my career." Even James Whale wasn't certain how the public would react to *Frankenstein*. He wanted the preview to be screened out of town so if the film did poorly, the word-of-mouth wouldn't be too strong. The preview was held at the Granada Theater in Santa Barbara on October 29, two days before Halloween.

James Whale's companion David Lewis, who attended the screening with the director, remembered, "... In 1931, this was awfully strong stuff. As it progressed, people got up, walked out, came back in, walked out again. It was an alarming thing." When *Frankenstein* ended with the deaths of Frankenstein and the monster, no one applauded. The preview cards were discouraging. One said, "Story is about a man who was destroyed by his own creation. Look out this doesn't happen to Universal." One filmgoer was so upset by *Frankenstein* that he telephoned the Granada Theater Manager at two in the morning. "I can't sleep," he bemoaned, "so I'm darned if you're going to sleep either!"

Both James Whale and Junior Laemmle panicked. They knew that if *Frankenstein* flopped, they would take the blame. They hastily devised and filmed an epilogue, in which Frankenstein is recovering. Colin Clive was unavailable because he was on a ship bound for Europe. Whale used a long shot for an unidentified actor.

Had Clive been in Hollywood, he wouldn't have been happy doing the epilogue. Unaware of the last-minute revisions, he told a reporter in New York City, "I think *Frankenstein* has an intense dramatic quality . . . and culminates when I, in the title role, am killed by the monster that I have created. This is a rather unusual ending for a talking picture, as the producers usually prefer that . . . [the story] . . . end happily with the hero and heroine clasped in each other's arms."

Universal also added a slightly tongue-in-cheek prologue to the film. The released film opens with Edward Van Sloan emerging from behind a curtain. "Mr. Carl Laemmle [Sr.] feels that it would be a little unkind to present this picture without just a word of friendly warning," he begins. Van Sloan briefly sums up *Frankenstein*'s premise. He concludes, "I think it will thrill you. It may shock you. It might even—horrify you. So if any of you feel that you do not care to subject your nerves to such a strain, now's your chance to ...uh...well, we warned you." As James Whale's biographer James Curtis points out, Van Sloan's introduction was "shrewdly worded to imply that refunds would be made at the door without actually saying as much. It also had the effect of ratcheting up the audience's expectations before a single frame of the story unfolded."

W.H. Wilkerson didn't find *Frankenstein* too frightening in his review in the *Hollywood Reporter:* "This is not an easy thing to direct—just how far to go in playing upon an audience's credulity, its sympathy, its nerves. Whale seems to have gone far enough, but not too far." But Leo Meehan in the *Motion Picture Herald* was aghast: *"Frankenstein* is a thriller, make no mistake. Women come out trembling, men exhausted. I don't know what it might do to children, but I know I wouldn't want my kids to see it." He especially was revolted by the drowning scene: "It is too dreadfully brutal, no matter what the story calls for. It carries gruesomeness and cruelty a little beyond reason or necessity."

Meehan's indignant reaction could not prevent people from seeing *Frankenstein*. The film set house records in various cities throughout the nation. Even in Chicago, it broke an attendance record, despite being billed for "adults only." Publicity emphasized *Frankenstein*'s chills: "To see it is to wear a badge of courage!" However, some communities considered the movie too chilling for suitable viewing. It was actually banned in small towns in Massachusetts. Several states scissored out elements in *Frankenstein* before releasing it.

The Kansas State Board of Censors made thirty-one cuts to the film, claiming that *Frankenstein* "tended to debase morals." Junior Laemmle was enraged; these cuts made the film incomprehensible. He persuaded Jason Joy to intervene on Universal's behalf. Joy telephoned the Kansas state censors, convincing them to restore some of the censored footage.

When *Frankenstein* was rereleased in 1938, Universal removed the segment of the monster throwing Maria into the water. For nearly half a century, this segment remained missing from circulating prints. Tom Johnson points out that since the lake scene ended with the monster reaching out for the girl, this may have inadvertently implied an even worse fate for her. In an interview for the horror magazine *Famous Monsters of Filmland*, Mae Clarke said, "Through NOT showing how ... [Maria died] ... pictorially and what ... [the monster's] ... reactions were, you missed the whole pathos—and this was unintentional." In 1985, a trim of the deleted segment was discovered and restored.

Frankenstein remains a riveting film today, due to Whale's atmospheric direction and Karloff's extraordinary performance. But its shocks, which rattled Depression-era viewers, now seem quite tame. Twice when the monster attacks Frankenstein, he bloodies his face slightly, but otherwise the violence is subtly handled. Whale doesn't depict the monster's murdering Fritz. Frankenstein and Dr. Waldman (Edward Van Sloan) hear the assistant's screams in another room. When they enter the room where Fritz has been killed, they see his suspended corpse. Whale depicts the corpse in a darkly-lit long shot, obscuring its features. The monster's strangulation of Dr. Waldman is brief and bloodless.

When the monster sees Frankenstein's fiancée Elizabeth (Mae Clarke), he only growls. The woman goes into shock, but only because she is startled by his hideous appearance. Mae Clarke looks elegant in her bridal grown, with a hint of exposed cleavage. In the post-Code era, the censors would have insisted that Clarke's entire bosom be concealed.

Frankenstein's popularity demonstrated that horror films were here to stay. Other studios decided to make chillers to rival Universal's. Paramount had the rights to another classic mad scientist story, Robert Louis Stevenson's *The Strange Case of Dr. Jekyll and Mr. Hyde*. The studio had already made a successful silent version starring John Barrymore. Now they proceeded to make their sound version. It would make *Frankenstein* seem genteel by comparison.

DR. JEKYLL AND MR. HYDE (1931)

Released December 31, 1931; A Rouben Mamoulian Production; Released by Paramount; *Director and Producer:* **Rouben Mamoulian;** *Screenplay:* **Samuel Hoffenstein and Percy Heath;** *Based on the novella* **The Strange Case of Dr. Jekyll and Mr. Hyde** *by Robert Louis Stevenson; Photography:* **Karl Struss;** *Art Director:* **Hans Dreier;** *Editor:* **William Shea;** *Makeup:* **Wally Westmore; 98 minutes.**

Cast: **Fredric March (Dr. Henry Jekyll/Mr. Hyde), Miriam Hopkins (Ivy Pierson), Rose Hobart (Muriel Carew), Holmes Herbert (Dr. Lanyon), Halliwell Hobbes (Brigadier-General Carew), Edgar Norton (Poole), Tempe Pigott (Mrs. Hawkins), Arnold Lucy (Utterson), Colonel MacDonnell (Hobson).**

SYNOPSIS: *In late nineteenth-century London, the kindly and respected Dr. Henry Jekyll lectures a group of scientists about the duality of the human psyche, opining that man deals with an eternal struggle between his noble and savage sides. Dr. Jekyll is working on a formula that will separate the two sides so the dark side can emerge and be annihilated. Engaged to marry Muriel Carew, the young doctor asks her father Brigadier-General Carew to move up the wedding date, but Carew refuses. Later, Jekyll completes and takes the formula, which releases his beastly side, Mr. Hyde. Hyde terrorizes Ivy Pierson, a working-class girl that Jekyll had earlier rescued from an assailant. When Hyde turns back into Jekyll, the remorseful scientist vows never to use the formula again and assures the frightened Ivy Hyde will never bother her again. Jekyll and Muriel persuade Carew to set an earlier wedding date, but on the night of the nuptial announcement, Jekyll involuntarily becomes Hyde and kills Ivy. Jekyll's colleague Dr. Lanyon witnesses Hyde reverting to Jekyll. Although shocked by the experiment, Lanyon swears to Jekyll he will not tell anybody else about it. Jekyll sorrowfully tells Muriel he is breaking their engagement as penance, but Hyde reemerges and murders Carew. When Lanyon learns of this, he leads the police to Jekyll's laboratory. There, the scientist has used the formula to return to normal, but when he sees Lanyon and the police, he turns to Hyde again and goes after them. The beast is shot and as he dies, he becomes Jekyll.*

In Robert Louis Stevenson's 1886 book, Mr. Hyde does not look *overtly* hideous. A "pale and dwarfish" figure, Hyde gives people "an impression of deformity without any nameable malformation." Dr. Jekyll's friend Mr. Utterson (an insignificant character in Mamoulian's film) speculates that Hyde's unsettling appearance is "the mere radiance of a foul soul that thus transpires through, and transfigures, its clay continent." Mr. Hyde is the manifestation of the dark side of Dr. Jekyll's personality. He repels everyone he sees because his character is thoroughly offensive.

Stevenson's deliberately-vague suggestion of Hyde's spiritual ugliness is chilling to read. A fiend whose horridness can only be sensed is more sinister than a physically-repulsive one. But this concept is only effective on the page; it is difficult to utilize it in the visual medium of film. Victor Fleming tried it with Spencer Tracy in the 1941 MGM version, but even without makeup, Hyde's nastiness was obvious, not subtle. Rouben Mamoulian wasn't interested in Stevenson's interpretation: "The original was about good and evil. Jekyll wanted to assume the different existence in order to commit acts of evil. I thought that was a very specific horror thing that the audience would hardly get involved with. I thought that if I changed that and made it a conflict not between good and evil but between the spiritual and the animal in man, that would be a part of every one of us."

In envisioning his concept of Dr. Jekyll's doppelganger, Mamoulian said, "As a prototype for Hyde, I didn't take a monster, but our common ancestor, the Neanderthal man. Mr. Hyde is not a monster but a primeval man—closest to the earth, the soil. When the first transformation takes place, Jekyll turns into Hyde, who is not the evil but the animal in him ... The first Hyde is this young animal released from the stifling manners and conventions of the Victorian period." The Victorian Era was a period of peace and prosperity for the British Empire under the long reign of Queen Victoria from 1837 until her death in 1901. It was also a time of rigid morality, when every respectable Britisher was expected to behave impeccably.

In subsequent transformations, Hyde becomes more cunning and dangerous. Every time Jekyll's bestial alter ego reemerges, he looks more gruesome. By the time of Hyde's last appearance, he appears to be in early stages of decay, with hollowed-out eyes. Hyde's facial deterioration is a frightening and effective device, dramatizing Jekyll's lessening control of his savage side. The makeup ordeal for Fredric March was torturous. Stage actress Rose Hobart, who played Jekyll's fiancée Muriel Carew, told interviewer Tom Weaver, "Of course, the worst thing to happen to Freddie on that picture was when the makeup man, who should have known better, was trying to make the masks, because Hyde got progressively worse. All of them were just too mask-like and Freddie couldn't move. So they made a mask and put it on Freddie with liquid rubber. He was in the hospital for three weeks! It took his whole face off! It was lucky he wasn't ruined for life! That's the kind of thing they used to do in those days and that's why I hated pictures! They didn't give a shit about people!" *Dr. Jekyll and Mr. Hyde* was filmed before the Screen Actors Guild was established. Had it been made when the union was active, Paramount would have probably been still rough on March, but the actor might have filed a grievance through the Guild. March himself joined the Guild shortly after its foundation in 1933 and contributed financially to the organization.

Whatever agonies March experienced on the set, they didn't affect his on-screen performance. Whether he is playing Dr. Jekyll or Mr. Hyde, the actor crackles with energy. March is particularly dynamic when his characters are aroused. In Stevenson's story, there was barely any hint of sex since literary censorship was quite strict in the late nineteenth century. But Rouben Mamoulian's film, even though its scenario takes place in the 1880s, radiates sensuality. Paramount's silent version of Stevenson's tale also explored Dr. Jekyll's libido, unleashed as his alter ego Mr. Hyde. But the studio's sound version makes its predecessor seem restrained by comparison.

Early in the film, Dr. Jekyll lectures at a university about his theory that people have two souls, a good one that "strives for the nobility" and a bad one that "seeks an expression of impulses that binds him to some dim animal relation with the earth... These two carry on an eternal struggle in the nature of man, yet they are chained together and that chain speaks repression to the evil, remorse to the good. Now, if these two selves could be separated from each other, how much freer the good in us would be. What heights it might scale and the so-called evil, once liberated, would fulfill itself and trouble us no more."

Film audiences soon learn about Jekyll's own struggle between civility and reckless abandon. Engaged to the attractive and vivacious Muriel Carew (Rose Hobart), he wants to marry her as soon as possible. But Muriel's straitlaced father Brigadier-General Carew (Halliwell Hobbes) objects to a hasty marriage. "I waited five years for your mother," he tells Muriel. "There's such a thing as decent observance, you know," he admonishes Jekyll.

Jekyll's conservative friend Dr. Lanyon (Holmes Herbert) agrees with Carew: "I hope the responsibilities of marriage will sober you up." "I'm not marrying to be sober. I'm marrying to be drunk. Drunk with life and experiments," Jekyll responds.

Soon the young doctor is tempted by another woman, the impetuous Ivy Pierson (Miriam Hopkins). She first attracts Jekyll's attention when she is assaulted by a man identified by an eyewitness as "one of Ivy Pearson's callers." (Another eyewitness scoffs that she had it coming to her.) Clearly a lady of the evening, Ivy dresses provocatively in low cut gowns. She plies her trade to sustain herself, living in a shabby flat that Hyde later derides as "that pigsty."

Infatuated by the handsome Jekyll, Ivy initiates the most brazen seduction sequence in American pre-Code horror cinema. Other pre-Codes like *Freaks* and *Supernatural* have sizzling seduction sequences, but none of the women in these films indulge in a striptease like Ivy does. Jason S. Joy, in a letter to Paramount associate producer B.P. Schulberg, opined that Ivy's disrobing scene seemed to be "dragged in simply to titillate the audience." Joy was mistaken;

the striptease sequence is crucial to *Jekyll and Hyde*'s scenario. It serves as character development for both Ivy and Jekyll. Ivy's playful undressing demonstrates her coarse, devil-may-care demeanor, unlike Muriel's refined, discreet deportment. Jekyll enthusiastically responds to her overtures, unleashing his repressed desires. The doctor would have engaged in sexual relations with Ivy had Lanyon not surprised them in a passionate embrace. The seduction scene foreshadows Hyde's enslavement of Ivy. He will subject her to verbal and physical abuse, venting all of Jekyll's pent-up rage until he ultimately kills her. This tragic outcome is further suggested when Jekyll debates with Lanyon. The straitlaced doctor admonishes his colleague for his dalliance with Ivy: "Perhaps you've forgotten you're engaged to Muriel." "Forgotten it?" Jekyll reacts. "Can a man dying of thirst forget water? Did you know what would happen to that thirst if it were denied water?"

Unlike the literary Jekyll, the scientist in Mamoulian's film doesn't initially take the potion to indulge himself in debauchery. Although he revels in his first transformation, he uses the drug to reverse the effects as soon as he hears his butler Poole (Edgar Norton) calling for him. Only when Jekyll learns that Muriel's father decides to take her on a trip to France does the doctor use the formula to act out his dark urges.

And what dark urges! Even by today's standards, the scenes of Hyde's tormenting Ivy are hard to watch. The actors' performances intensify the horror—March as the sadistic Hyde and Hopkins as the terrified Ivy. Despite his outlandish makeup, March's brutality is harrowingly real. Hopkins' fright, particularly evident in her wide eyes, is also uncomfortably convincing. Hyde cruelly forces Ivy to sing for him. "Sing, my little pigeon! Get up and sing! You hear?" he commands Ivy. His savage tone is dark with unspeakable threat. Intimidated, she starts to warble, in a shaky voice, a suggestive tune: "Champagne Ivy is my name / Good for any game at night, my boys." But she cannot really sing; she shudders, voice and body trembling. Unable to finish, Ivy collapses in tears.

Tom Johnson in *Censored Screams: The British Ban on Hollywood Horror in the Thirties* points out that Hyde's sexual torture of Ivy would probably not be filmed in a non-horror film. He opines, "... if

Hyde were just an 'ordinary man,'... [the abuse] would be unbearable in its realism." Mark A. Vieira in *Sin in Soft Focus: Pre-code Hollywood* points out that Hyde's scenes with Ivy smack of bestiality; Jekyll's doppelganger is supposed to be a Neanderthal man. Significantly, Ivy calls Hyde a "beast." Paramount would later go farther with bestiality in the chiller *The Island of Lost Souls*. The studio would also depict sexual sadism more bluntly in *Murders in the Zoo*.

Hyde's murder of Ivy occurs off screen. But the filmgoers hear his words as he kills her: "There, my sweet. There, my love. There, my little bride. Isn't Hyde a lover after your own heart?" As the murder takes place, a copy of Antonio Canova's sculpture of the mythical lovers Cupid and Psyche appears in the foreground. It's a stylish and imaginative concept, but the symbolism is audacious. Would this device have been permitted under the strengthened Code? Perhaps, since James Whale got away with outrageous images like a crucified Frankenstein Monster in the post-Code *The Bride of Frankenstein.*

Hyde's killing of Carew is also carnally motivated. Alone with Lanyon, Jekyll fumes over Carew's refusal to move up the wedding date: "It's a pity I didn't strangle the old walrus! Did you hear him? 'Wait!' What the devil does one wait for?" As Hyde, he beats Carew to death with the cane when the old man stops him from menacing Muriel. Mamoulian depicts the bludgeoning discreetly, showing only Hyde wielding his cane. Hyde's fatal shooting is also handled with restraint; there is no visible bloodshed.

If Mr. Hyde is a more erotic monster in Mamoulian's film than he is in Stevenson's story, then Dr. Jekyll is portrayed as a more romantic and tragic figure. The literary Dr. Jekyll is "a large, well-made, smooth-faced man of fifty." His doppelganger Hyde is not only conscienceless but youthful. Jekyll's motives to create a different personality are egoistic: as Hyde, he can revel in debaucheries without worrying he'll tarnish Jekyll's impeccable reputation. The doctor soon learns he cannot control his dark side and he rues his experiment. But if Jekyll regrets the evil he does, he doesn't say so. In his confessional testament, written just before he kills himself, Jekyll only laments that his experiment in the human psyche has failed and he cannot rid himself of Mr. Hyde. Jekyll remains in a prison of his own making.

Rouben Mamoulian decided that his Dr. Jekyll should be a young man because the director believed "rebellion and transformation is more interesting when it is the result of the ferment of youthful aspirations." Jekyll's sexual desires are shown as the normal passions of an individual in the bloom of manhood. Filmgoers could empathize with his ardor for his fiancée Muriel and his eagerness to marry her. They could also understand Ivy's attraction to him. Like Bela Lugosi's Dracula, Fredric March's Jekyll was an alluring and dashing figure. The public could more easily identify with him than with Stevenson's middle-aged Jekyll.

Before March was cast in *Dr. Jekyll and Mr. Hyde*, he had a reputation as a romantic lead and as a light comedian. Paramount cast him as a leading man for the studio's female stars like Ruth Chatterton and Claudette Colbert. March had already received an Oscar nomination as Tony Cavendish, a lampoon of John Barrymore, in *The Royal Family* (1930). Paramount's studio head Adolph Zukor wanted dour looking character-actor Irving Pichel to play Jekyll and Hyde. Pichel had recently played a homicidal halfwit in the suspense film *Murder by the Clock* (1931).

Mamoulian objected to Zukor's choice: ". . . Irving Pichel might have been suited to the doctor as he was written in the novel, but I knew he was completely inappropriate for the film." The Paramount brass agreed with Mamoulian that Dr. Jekyll should be virile and handsome, and suggested juvenile leading man Phillips Holmes in the title roles. Mamoulian felt that Holmes would make a believable Jekyll but an unconvincing Hyde. The director was convinced only Fredric March could tackle both roles. The film's enormous success and March's Oscar for Best Actor vindicated the director's choice.

In the film, as soon as Jekyll learns that Muriel and her father are returning from France, he vows never to torment Ivy again. At first, he assumes he can mollify Ivy with money. She fears that Hyde will return, and she visits the doctor hoping he'll protect her. Ivy is convinced she can't tell the police about Hyde: "Who cares what becomes of the likes of me?" Ivy feels the authorities won't help her because she is a streetwalker. Jekyll is horrified and remorseful when Ivy pours out to him her anguish and shows him Hyde's whip marks on her back (concealed from the filmgoers.) Realizing that Ivy doesn't want money but emotional reassurance, he swears to her, "I give you my word that you will never be troubled with Hyde again."

After Jekyll involuntarily reverts to Hyde, kills Ivy, and becomes Jekyll again, the scientist prays: "I saw a light, but I could not see where it was leading. I have trespassed on your domain. I've gone further than man should go. Forgive me. Help me." For of all *Dr. Jekyll and Mr. Hyde*'s raciness and edginess, this scene affirms traditional Judeo-Christian morality. Convinced that his soul has been damned for eternity, Jekyll visits Muriel to renounce their relationship. "I give you up because I love you so," he mournfully declares. "This is my proof. This is my penance." But Jekyll cannot give up his demonic alter ego, and only death can destroy Mr. Hyde. In Stevenson's story, Jekyll dies as Hyde, the evil doppelganger having completely taking over his body. But in Mamoulian's film, when Hyde perishes, he turns back into Dr. Jekyll. Filmgoers are reassured that Jekyll's demise signifies the end of his evil side.

Despite the film's nod to orthodox values, it casts a cold eye on Victorian society. Dr. Lanyon constantly admonishes Dr. Jekyll for his scientific ventures. He senses that his friend is toying with fate. But Lanyon's aversion to scientific tampering isn't just motivated by prudence but by a resistance to change. In advocating his exploration of hidden knowledge, Jekyll alludes to a gas lamp in the streets: "But for some man's curiosity, we shouldn't have had it. London would still be lighted by linkboys. And wait. One day, London will glow with incandescence . . . and will be so beautiful that even you will be moved by it." Lanyon demurs, "I find London quite satisfactory as it is and I'm not interested in your shortcuts and your byways." Lanyon is much older than Jekyll, which may explain his hidebound conservatism. Unlike Dr. Jekyll, the elder doctor is a narrow-minded snob who values empty protocol above all. Lanyon is annoyed with Jekyll for skipping a meeting with a Duchess in order to care for his needy patients: "You know how insistent the Duchess was on your coming. You can't neglect her for a lot of charity cases." He becomes irritated when Jekyll misses dinner at General Carew's estate to operate on an impoverished patient.

General Carew shares Lanyon's insular attitudes. When Lanyon tells him that Jekyll won't be coming to dinner, he says, "I hope the patient is worthy of Jekyll's attention." Learning that Jekyll is working in the free ward, Carew scornfully says, "Free ward!" as if it is a dump that no gentleman should even enter. When Jekyll arrives after the dinner to dance with Muriel and apologizes for his tardiness, Carew says, "Repentance is a virtue, Jekyll, but it's better to be punctual."

Eventually Carew gives his consent to Jekyll and Muriel for an early marriage. But when Jekyll unwillingly becomes Hyde and misses his formal engagement announcement, the old man tells his daughter, "I forbid you to see this man again." Muriel, who has defended Jekyll in the past, is defiant: "You've never understood him and never tried to understand him. You tried to bend him to your will. I haven't fought for him. I don't know what's happened to him, but I know he's suffering, and it's our fault, mine more than yours."

After seeing the completed cut of *Dr. Jekyll and Mr. Hyde*, Jason S. Joy opined, "Because it is so well established a literary classic the public and the censors may overlook the horrors which result from the realism of the Hyde makeup though we [the Production Code] cannot estimate what the reaction will be to this . . . Certainly we hope that excellence of the production will offset any apprehension that the theme is too harrowing."

The Production Code's hope was fulfilled. *Dr. Jekyll and Mr. Hyde* was both a commercial and a critical success. The film was featured in both *Film Daily* and *The New York Times*' "Ten Best" lists. Not only did Fredric March win an Oscar, but Percy Heath and Samuel Hoffenstein were nominated for Best Screenplay and Karl Struss for Best Cinematography. (Both nominations were deserved.) The film not only boosted Fredric March's career but Miriam Hopkins' as well. Throughout the next few years of the pre-Code period, she was cast as free-spirited women in such films as Ernst Lubitsch's comedies *Trouble in Paradise* (1932) and *Design for Living* (1933). Her most notorious pre-Code part would be the title role of a debutante who suffers a brutal assault in *The Story of Temple Drake* (1933), adapted from William Faulkner's novel *Sanctuary*.

Movie theaters exploited *Dr. Jekyll and Mr. Hyde*'s horror angle. *The Motion Picture Herald* reported that one theater in Long Branch, New Jersey provided the local paper with a "Fear Moment" stunt in connection with the film. The readers were asked to write an account of the most fearsome experience in their life and submit it to the paper. Ten of the contributors were awarded guest tickets for the picture. *The Film Daily* noted that another theater in Texarkana, Texas cooperated with the local paper for another publicity stunt. One man and one woman each were offered $2.50 if both of them sat through a midnight showing prior to the film's official opening, with the man on one side of the theater auditorium and the woman on the other side. Both people selected for the midnight screening had to be physically examined and sign a waiver releasing the theater from all responsibility!

Despite *Dr. Jekyll and Mr. Hyde*'s popularity, some people felt it was unsuitable for younger viewers. Guy Jones reported in *The Motion Picture Herald* that Ralph Stitt, who ran the Rivoli Theatre in New York, New York, used the film's trailer as a coming attraction. The main feature was *Sooky*, starring child actor Jackie Cooper, which attracted a young audience. Worried that the juvenile patrons would find the trailer too terrifying, Stitt came up with an advance trailer to precede *Jekyll*'s with the warning: "Notice to Adults and Children at this performance. The following sequences announcing the future presentation of 'DR. JEKYLL AND MR. HYDE' are rather strong dramatically. We recommend that juvenile attention be diverted from the screen for the next few moments. The management." Guy Jones advised other cinema managers: "We pass this on to you, boys, because it can be used in connection with any trailer that requires it."

At least one person who saw it considered Rouben Mamoulian's film morally enlightening. Miriam Miller in Washington, D.C. wrote in the "What the Audience Thinks" column in *Photoplay*:

"Many years I have attended my church faithfully, but never before has a sermon on 'the wages of sin is death' been brought to me so forcefully as it was in the phonoplay 'Dr. Jekyll and Mr. Hyde.'

Here I saw portrayed vividly the result of one following his baser impulses and the effect not only on himself, but upon those with whom he came in contact. I came away from the picture feeling that I had been taught a spiritual lesson."

This quote may help explain why *Dr. Jekyll and Mr. Hyde* was not only a critical hit but resulted in Fredric March's Oscar and other Oscar nominations. The staid Academy for the Motion Pictures Arts and Sciences was generally snobbish about horror films. None of the other chillers released between 1931 and 1934 received any nominations, let alone awards. Charles Laughton won the 1932-33 Oscar as Best Actor for *The Private Life of Henry the Eighth* but he wasn't even nominated for *The Island of Lost Souls*, released in the same period.

Dr. Jekyll and Mr. Hyde played in cinemas for a long time but it was cut in later showings. The trims were probably not done to remove potentially offensive material but so theater managers could squeeze in extra showings for patrons. The film's original running time was unusually long for a 1931 feature. *Variety's* reviewer opined, "It runs overtime on footage. Labored adornment of the original simplicity weakens the production for mob appeal. High pitch of emotional horror is difficult to maintain beyond some certain degree of elapsed time, and the 98 minutes this picture runs carries it past the human limit." Rouben Mamoulian's entire film would disappear from public view for a long time. In 1941, Metro-Goldwyn-Mayer bought the film's rights from Paramount to remake it with Spencer Tracy in the title roles. To avoid comparisons with the earlier version, MGM banished the 1931 prints to the vaults. In the late 1960s, Raymond Rohauer discovered a copy of the Mamoulian film, and it was subsequently shown on television and in revival theaters. Today it is commercially available on home video.

At the time of *Dr. Jekyll and Mr. Hyde*'s release in 1932, Universal planned a new horror film. Like *Dr. Jekyll and Mr. Hyde*, this film was an adaption of a classic story, Edgar Allan Poe's "Murders in the Rue Morgue." Little of Poe's tale would survive Universal's version. Instead it would be a showcase for Bela Lugosi, a follow up to his triumph in *Dracula*. And it would dwell on bestiality, a controversial subject avoided in Poe's narrative.

MURDERS IN THE RUE MORGUE [1932]

Released February 10, 1932; A Universal Picture; *Director:* Robert Florey; *Producer:* Carl Laemmle, Jr.; *Associate Producer:* E.M. Asher; *Screenplay:* Tom Reed and Dale Van Every; *Based on the story* "The Murders of the Rue Morgue" *by Edgar Allan Poe; Adaptation:* Robert Florey; *Additional Dialogue:* John Huston; *Scenario Editor:* Richard Schayer; *Photography:* Karl Freund; *Art Director:* Charles D. Hall; *Editor:* Milton Carruth; *Supervising Editor:* Maurice Pivar; *Musical Director:* Heinz Roemheld; *Special Effects:* John P. Fulton; *Makeup:* Jack P. Pierce; 62 minutes.

Cast: Sidney Fox (Mlle. Camille L'Espanaye), Bela Lugosi (Dr. Mirakle), Leon Waycoff [Ames] (Pierre Dupin), Bert Roach (Paul), Betsy Ross Clarke (Mme. L'Espanaye), Brandon Hurst (Prefect of Police), D'Arcy Corrigan (Morgue Keeper), Noble Johnson (Janos, the Black One), Arlene Francis (Woman of the Streets), Charles Gemora (Erik the Ape).

SYNOPSIS: *In 1845 Paris, scientist Dr. Mirakle displays a gorilla named Erik at a carnival as proof that people are descended from apes. He declares he can prove it by mixing the primate's blood with man's. After the carnival ends, Mirakle and his assistant Janos abduct a woman of the streets to subject her to his experiment. But the woman, whose blood is diseased, dies after Mirakle injects Erik's blood sample into her, and the doctor disposes of her corpse in the river. Her corpse is discovered by others and sent to the morgue; she is Mirakle's third victim this week. When medical student Pierre Dupin, who earlier saw Mirakle at the carnival, learns of this, he bribes the morgue keeper for a sample of the woman's blood. Dupin discovers that all three women died from a "foreign" substance injected into their blood. The student is engaged to Camille L'Espanaye and Erik, who saw her at the carnival, is attracted to her. Mirakle, with Erik's assistance, abducts Camille to use in his experiment. Dupin, who has deduced that the "foreign" substance is gorilla blood and recognizes Mirakle's scheme, alerts the police about this and they storm Mirakle's laboratory. Erik, infatuated with Camille, kills Mirakle and carries her off on the rooftops. Dupin shoots Erik and rescues Camille while Mirakle's corpse ends up at the morgue.*

Universal was determined to capitalize on *Dracula* and *Frankenstein*'s success with a new chiller. A faithful adaptation of Edgar Allan Poe's 1841 short story "The Murders in the Rue Morgue" was out of the question. Poe's original tale has horrific elements, particularly gruesome killings, but it is actually a detective story. Poe focuses on sleuth C. Auguste Dupin's efforts to deduce the killer's identity. In adapting the story to the screen, Robert Florey changed it from a murder mystery to a mad doctor chiller. Universal's new horror star Bela Lugosi was cast as the twisted Dr. Mirakle, a character invented for the film.

Florey later recalled, "In *Rue Morgue* I used the same device I employed in my Frankenstein adaptation. Bela Lugosi became Dr. Mirakle—a mad scientist desirous of creating a human being—not with body parts stolen from a graveyard and a brain from a lab, but the mating of an ape with a woman." Poe's primate, an animal who flees his human master to wreak havoc in the story, became Mirakle's guinea pig in the doctor's diabolical experiment. Florey's concept of bestiality was toned down in a revised draft and replaced by the mixing of human and ape blood.

Dr. Mirakle's perverse plan to provide a human lover for his gorilla Erik is still obvious. Injecting simian blood into the unfortunate prostitute (Arlene Francis, years before she became a glamorous regular on the popular TV quiz show *What's My Line?*), the fiendish doctor declares his intentions: "If you only last one more minute, then we shall see—we shall know if you are to be the bride of science!" He obsessively examines his female victims' blood samples to see if they are positive for venereal disease. Enraged at what he sees in the microscope, Mirakle screams at the dying woman, "Your blood is rotten! Black as your sins! You cheated me! Your beauty was a lie!" Later, after abducting the virginal Camille (Sidney Fox), he studies her sample and exults, "Her blood is perfect!" Mirakle has no carnal interest in the women; he only wants to use them to validate his theory of the kinship between people and apes.

The moment Erik (Charles Gemora) sets his eyes on Camille, he is consumed by lust. He snatches the bonnet from her head. Had the gorilla not been caged, he might have ripped off her clothes; he caresses Camille's bonnet with passionate curiosity. Grinning wickedly, Dr. Mirakle tells the startled woman, "Erik is only human, Mademoiselle. He has an eye for beauty." The aroused ape won't tolerate any human competitors; he tries to strangle her fiancé Pierre Dupin (Leon Ames).

Mirakle orders the ape to leave Pierre alone. But just as Dr. Frankenstein could not control his monster, this scientist cannot control his ape. Unlike the monster, Erik kills Mirakle. In the climax, the uncaged gorilla is so infatuated with Camille he sees Mirakle as an intrusive rival. Mirakle is not only punished for tampering with science but for his hubris in trying to control a wild animal. Eric Gorman in *Murders in the Zoo* also believes he can dominate his menagerie of beasts, but one of them destroys him. Carl Denham in *King Kong* suffers the same delusion in his handling of King Kong, but he is spared because he doesn't *intentionally* use the creature to hurt or kill people.

If Dr. Mirakle transgresses the bounds of decency of trying to crossbreed an ape with a human, he is on the right track in his theory that people evolved from apes. (The doctor publicly declares this in 1845 Paris, fourteen years before Charles Darwin revealed his theory of evolution in *The Origin of Species*.) When an elderly carnival spectator rises from his seat and shouts, "Heresy!" Mirakle replies sardonically, "Heresy. Heresy. Do they still burn men for heresy? Then burn me, Monsieur. Light the fire. Do you still think your little candle will outshine the flame of truth?" Unlike the aged protester, Pierre Dupin does not dismiss Mirakle's scientific concept. Dupin's buffoonish roommate Paul (Bert Roach, intended as comic relief from *Rue Morgue*'s gruesome scenario) scoffs at evolution. But

Pierre says to his friend, "Has it occurred to you that he might be right?"

Pierre Dupin, like Dr. Mirakle, studies scientific mysteries. In discovering startling theories and facts, he challenges the status quo. But unlike Mirakle, Dupin has a strong ethical sense. He will not sacrifice human lives in his quest for knowledge. He especially reveals his concern for human life in the climax. When Erik runs off with Camille, Pierre stops a gendarme from shooting the ape. The young man realizes the lawman might accidentally kill the girl. Pierre himself vanquishes the ape and rescues his fiancée. (Why isn't Dupin concerned about Erik's life? Because the ape is an uncontrollable and dangerous creature who wants to ravage Camille.)

Pierre is not above breaking the law in order to obtain the desired knowledge. He bribes the morgue keeper (D'Arcy Corrigan) to send him the prostitute's corpse so he can determine the cause of her death. Michael Brunas, John Brunas, and Tom Weaver point out in *Universal Horrors* that religious symbolism is used ironically: "The oversized wooden cross in the morgue bears witness to the shady dealings of the coroner, who flagrantly accepts bribes of medical students as leering attendants bring in the bodies of murdered women of the night." The coroner is never caught; in the final scene, he examines Mirakle's corpse.

Not all of *Rue Morgue*'s Christian imagery is ironic. Camille wears a cross around her neck, symbolizing her virtue, which is emphasized in a scene just before her kidnapping, when she prays before a crucifix. Curiously, the prostitute wears a cross around her neck. Could her wearing of the cross signify her shame or her desire for salvation? Even before Mirakle abducts her, she is obviously troubled, weeping at the sight of two men killing each other over her.

Rue Morgue's mid-nineteenth century setting is appropriate. The theory of evolution wouldn't seem outrageous in a 1930s milieu. But when production began, Universal objected to spending extra money for period props and costumes. The studio, plagued by financial problems and worried about budget overruns, wanted to give the film a contemporary setting. Robert Florey walked off the lot in protest. Rather than searching for another director, the studio permitted him to use a historical backdrop to shoot *Rue Morgue*.

After Florey finished the production on November 13, 1931, Universal brought him, the cast, and crew for retakes and additional scenes. *Frankenstein* had just been released and was doing sensational business. Carl Laemmle, Jr. was determined to polish up *Rue Morgue* to make it a profitable shocker like *Frankenstein*.

Less than a year before *Rue Morgue*'s release, Universal distributed *The Mystery of Life*, an educational film about evolution. Clarence Darrow, who had defended John T. Scopes for teaching Darwin's theory in a Tennessee school in 1925, narrated and appeared in this documentary. The New York State Board of Censors did not object to the film's Darwinian premise, but it scissored out material it considered obscene, such as babies on their mothers' breasts and copulating animals. Darrow protested the cuts: "Absurd and the censors know it ... Pictures of the Holy Mother nursing her infant abound all over the world ... The story of the praying mantis is published everywhere ... The human embryo is in any number of textbooks... ." On appeal, the censors restored most of the "objectionable" material before releasing it in New York. But fundamentalist Christians protested the film; the local association of ministers in Dayton, Tennessee denounced it as "anti-Biblical and anti-Christian," and demanded a boycott. One can only wonder of their reactions if they had seen *Murders in the Rue Morgue*.

The Production Code Administration (PCA) expressed concerns about *Rue Morgue* during production. It wasn't offended by the film's motif of blood mingling, but it objected to the scenes with the skimpily-dressed dancing women in the carnival and the "crucifixion" of Arlene Francis. Universal ignored the Code's complaints. The dancing women segment is a brazen example of pre-Code cinema. What makes it outrageous are the spectators' comments. One lecherous old man asks another codger, "Do they bite?" His friend replies, "Oh yes. But you have to pay extra for that." Camille wonders, "See Pierre how brown they are. Is that their real color, do you suppose, or have they painted themselves?" Her fiancé teases her: "Shall I find out for you?" In contrast to the prim and proper male romantic leads in other pre-Code horrors, particularly David Manners' characters, Pierre has a sense of racy humor.

Arlene Francis' "crucifixion" scene is indisputably *Rue Morgue*'s most unsettling sequence. The sight of her trussed up on a tilted cross in torn mid-nineteenth century undergarments to be tested as a potential mate for Erik is sacrilegious. What makes the scene so disturbing is Francis' anguish and Mirakle's callousness. As she wails piteously, the mad doctor angrily orders her, "Hush!" He then grins fiendishly, his eyes gleaming with diabolical intent as he injects the ape's blood into her arm. Mirakle doesn't consider her a human being, just an experimental subject.

When Francis expires, the grief-stricken Mirakle falls to his knees before her. The image of the scientist clasping his hands as if in prayer is even more blasphemous. Is Mirakle truly remorseful, or is he disappointed that the prostitute can't be used as the gorilla's partner? Whatever the reason, the sinister scientist quickly recovers, coldly telling his assistant Janos (Noble Johnson), "Get rid of it." The assistant cuts the rope with an axe, causing the dead woman to fall through a trap door into the river Seine. Mirakle declaims, "Will my search never end?" Lugosi's melodramatic delivery brings this bizarre scene to a close.

Francis herself, rather than a stuntwoman, fell into the water. She later recalled to David J. Skal in *The Monster Show* that Universal expected her to swim: "I couldn't even float, but I kept my mouth shut." She practiced floating in a friend's pool "until I was blue and waterlogged." In later years, Francis could laugh about the "crucifixion" scene. She gave Mr. Skal a still of the scene with the inscription "Don't ever do this to anybody you like." Robert Florey intended the spectacle of Francis's plight to be the first scene in *Murders in the Rue Morgue*. The scene would establish Mirakle's frantic search for the perfect human partner of his ape. The carnival segment where Mirakle and Erik first meet Camille was supposed to follow that; the doctor, recognizing the ape's attraction to her, would resolutely pursue the innocent woman to accomplish his experiment. But Universal decided that Francis' sequence was too horrific an opening for box office patrons. The released film started with the relatively light-hearted carnival episode, followed by the "crucifixion" sequence.

This version has remained in film revivals, on television screenings, and on commercial home video. But the film's dramatic significance has been diminished. By starting with the carnival and then proceeding to Arlene Francis's scene, the viewer assumes the prostitute distracts Mirakle from his quest for Camille. Had *Rue Morgue* been released in its original form, the doctor's attraction to Camille would have had greater impact; her innocence contrasts with the prostitute's tainted reputation. The studio's juggling of sequences also muddles the film's continuity. In the released version, Mirakle arrives with Erik in a coach to Camille's residence. The night is clear. He gets out without the ape, and the coach drives off. Suddenly, the night is dense with fog. Mirakle reappears in the coach but without Erik. Chicago's censor board made some cuts in the film before showing it in the city. The same New York State Board of Censors that deleted "obscene" elements of *The Mystery of Life* removed most of Arlene Francis' footage from *Rue Morgue* before letting it be shown. But New York City's Mayfair Theatre depicted a life-size cutout of Lugosi kneeling before the "crucified" Francis in its lobby. Arlene's father, New York portrait photographer Aram Kazanjian, was appalled. He rushed a telegram to her in Hollywood: I HAVE SEEN YOU HALF NAKED ON BROADWAY STOP OUR FRIENDS HAVE SEEN YOU TOO STOP COME HOME AT ONCE. Arlene phoned him to explain. Aram demanded she call the Mayfair Theatre to remove the offending cutout. Arlene reluctantly agreed. She knew she was wasting her time; she heard laughter on the receiving end.

Robert Florey, with assistance from cinematographer Karl Freund, adeptly handles the actual murders in *Rue Morgue* with style and discretion. In dramatizing Erik's killing of Camille's mother (Betsy Ross Clarke), the director doesn't show the body. The audience only hears Madame L'Espanaye's groan to convey the brutality. Silhouettes are used to illustrate Erik's murder of Mirakle. Edgar G. Ulmer would later use this technique in *The Black Cat* when Vitus Werdegast skins Hjalmar Poelzig alive. When Janos is shot by the police and Erik is shot by Pierre, neither of the victims are shown shedding blood.

Rue Morgue's horrors did not impress all the critics. *Variety* commented, "'Dracula' and 'Frankenstein' having softened them up, this third of U's [Universal's] baby-scaring cycle won't have the benefit of shocking them stiff and making them talk about it. Had it come first there's no doubt it would have created a stronger impression." Charles E. Lewis advised cinema owners in *Motion Picture Herald*, "In the title you have a powerful selling slant but we hardly advise anything like your 'Frankenstein' campaign for this one. Don't warn them about not seeing it if they have weak hearts ... There is not as much fast action and thrills as might have been expected. I found it mild entertainment."

Some filmgoers found *Rue Morgue* too silly to be frightening. *Variety* wrote, "At the Mayfair a cynical audience hooted the final hokum...." *The New York Times* reported a similar reaction at the Mayfair: "The crowning spectacle of the ape clambering over the Paris roofs with the unconscious Camille on its arm brought some irreverent squeals from last night's audience." Lonnie Noll, a Chicago patron, wrote to *Picture Play*, "... as for 'Murders in the Rue Morgue,' it was pathetic. Bela Lugosi should be ashamed of himself—the big tease! Mr. Lugosi, a group of children seated in front of me at the theater laughed every time a close-up of you was shown. One seven-year-old boy said he thought you must have a pain to make those faces." Lugosi would have been mortified if he had been at the screening. Huntz Hall, who worked with Lugosi in two comedies in the 1940s, recalled about the Hungarian actor, "He loved to laugh, but not to be laughed at. That would make him more angry than anything."

Despite some negative feedback, *Murders in the Rue Morgue* made money. Significantly, it didn't make as much as Universal's predecessors *Dracula* and *Frankenstein*. The studio would re-release it in 1936 with the "crucifixion" scene excised. Around the same time of *Rue Morgue*'s initial release, Metro-Goldwyn-Mayer jumped on the horror bandwagon. This studio would initially regret it. The film *Freaks* would arouse such condemnation in the press and rejection from the public that MGM would disown it. Americans found *Freaks too* scary to be entertaining. The film's malformed creatures, unlike the Frankenstein Monster and Mr. Hyde, were real.

FREAKS (1932)

Released February 20, 1932; A Metro-Goldwyn-Mayer Production; *Director:* **Tod Browning;** *Screenplay:* **Willis Goldbeck and Leon Gordon;** *Additional Dialogue:* **Edgar Allan Woolf and Al Boasberg;** *Suggested by the short story* **"Spurs"** *by Todd Robbins; Photography:* **Merrit B. Gerstad;** *Editor:* **Basil Wrangell; 64 minutes.**

Cast: **Wallace Ford (Phroso), Leila Hyams (Venus), Olga Baclanova (Cleopatra), Roscoe Ates (Roscoe), Henry Victor (Hercules), Harry Earles (Hans), Daisy Earles (Frieda), Rose Dione (Madame Tetrallini), Albert Conti (Monsieur Duval, the Landowner), Michael Visaroff (Jean, the Caretaker), Murray Kinnell (Sideshow Barker).**

SYNOPSIS: *At the carnival's sideshow, the barker introduces the aghast spectators to a shocking exhibit (the film audience doesn't see it), explaining she was once the beautiful and graceful trapeze artist Cleopatra. When the barker starts to explain how she became a "freak," the story proceeds to a flashback: One of the sideshow's dwarves, Hans, is infatuated with Cleopatra. His fiancée, the dwarf Frieda, is distressed because she knows that Cleopatra is toying with Hans's affections for her own sadistic amusement. When Hans breaks off his engagement to Frieda, she goes to Cleopatra to beg her to stop taking advantage of him. But when she mentions that Hans has inherited a fortune, Cleopatra and her strongman lover Hercules devise a scheme. The trapeze artist will marry Hans and then poison him so she can get his money and share it with Hercules. After the wedding, the other "freaks" treat the new couple to a feast. Enraged when the "freaks" declare her one of them, Cleopatra insults them and humiliates Hans by carrying him around on her shoulders. Shocked and offended, the "freaks" soon learn about Cleopa-*

tra and Hercules's scheme and alert Hans about it. One stormy night, they extract a gruesome revenge on Cleopatra, making her a "duck woman." They attack Hercules when he threatens the seal trainer Venus, who is a friend of the "freaks" and learns about the murder scheme. With the flashback over, the film audience sees the mutilated Cleopatra. Afterwords, Hans reunites with Frieda.

Irving Thalberg, MGM's dynamic executive in charge of production, told screenwriter Willis Goldbeck, "I want you to write me something even more horrible than *Dracula* or *Frankenstein*." After discussing the potential story with director Tod Browning, Goldbeck came up with the script for *Freaks*. When Thalberg read it, he shook his head and put his face in his hands: "I asked for something horrifying. Well, I got it." MGM's President Louis B. Mayer found it *too* horrifying and objected to its filming. Director Jack Conway stood up for Thalberg: "Irving's right so often he's earned the right to be wrong." Thalberg insisted on going ahead with the filming. The people were eagerly flooding the cinemas to see Universal and Paramount's horror films; why shouldn't MGM provide its own? Besides, Tod Browning had directed *Dracula*, and that film trailblazed the horror craze. Thalberg assured the worried Mayer, "If it's a mistake, I'll take the blame."

Freaks turned out to be a box office disaster. But it's not surprising that Tod Browning was attracted to its sawdust milieu. As a youth, he worked in a carnival troupe performing a variety of stunts like eating snakes and getting buried alive. Browning hung out with the sideshow "freaks," accepting them despite their physical defects. The director's earlier MGM films like *The Show* and *The Unknown* had carnival themes. Browning was also familiar with Tod Robbins's story "Spurs," which inspired *Freaks*'s screenplay. In fact, he had already directed a cinematic adaptation of another Tod Robbins story, *The Unholy Three* (1925). The midget Harry Earles had appeared in that film as a criminal masquerading as a baby. Earles was a friend of Browning's; the director cast him as the tragic Hans in *Freaks*. Harry's short-statured sister Daisy played Frieda, Hans' unrequited lover.

Although Browning was fascinated with "Spurs," he realized it lacked heart. In Robbins' original story, published in 1923, a voluptuous bareback rider marries a bad-humored circus midget after learning he has inherited a fortune. She thinks he'll die young because of his small stature. When she humiliates her new husband at the wedding feast, the vengeful dwarf makes her carry him on her back while he kicks her with spurs on his boots. The dwarf's dog, which he rides in the circus, snaps at her ankles. Robbins's story is a morbidly-fascinating read, but it lacks any likable characters.

The dwarf's character was sweetened in the screenplay. His name changed from Jacques to Hans (Harry Earles was from Germany), he was changed from a misanthrope to a guileless innocent. (But like his literary counterpart, he has a quick temper.) In order to make Hans even more sympathetic, the scenarists villified the full-sized circus performer, now a trapeze artist named Cleopatra (Olga Baclanova). In the film, she isn't content to wait for Hans to die; she tries to poison him. In a sense, she deserves her comeuppance, which is far more horrible than in the original story. Frieda was created in the screenplay to further endear Hans to filmgoers; this sweet midget loves him for who he is and doesn't care for his money.

The scenarists also concocted two decent "normal" characters as identification figures for filmgoers, Venus the seal trainer and Phroso the clown. Unlike Cleopatra and her strong man lover Hercules (Henry Victor) who conspires with her to kill Hans, Venus and Phroso are always kind and respectful toward the "freaks." But even though Venus and Phroso are attractive looking, they are both in a sense outcasts. Phroso (played by Wallace Ford in the film) hints he has a sexual problem. When Venus (Lelia Hyams), who is smitten by him, tells Phroso that he's a "good kid," he replies, "You're darn right I am. You shoulda caught me before my operation." Venus, although good at heart, does not adhere to polite society's rigid mores. Bryan Senn points out in *Golden Horrors:*

"The character of Venus is definitely not your standard chaste heroine ... We are introduced to her just as she leaves Hercules, obviously after having lived with him for some time. It's good to see that a 'fallen woman' (or 'tramp' as Hercules unfairly calls her) can be a likable protagonist and find happiness (even getting the guy) at the end ... One must be thankful that *Freaks* was filmed without the yoke of the Code, which undoubtedly would have demanded that her character be whitewashed and pure or alternatively would have required a messy end for her."

Why do Cleopatra and Hercules scorn the "freaks," even though they work in the circus with Venus and Phroso? A trapeze artist is a more prestigious position in the tent than a seal trainer. The barker (Murray Kinnell) in the opening scene says a prince shot himself out of love for Cleopatra. Hercules is a strong man who inspires awe, whereas Phoroso is a clown who is merely laughed at. It is no wonder that Cleopatra and Hercules are arrogant and selfish. And they suffer for their hubris in the end.

Cleopatra and Hercules express their mutual passion very crudely. After breaking an egg in a pan for the ravenous strong man, she says, "How do you like them?" As she speaks, Cleopatra thrusts out her chest. Hercules replies, "Not bad," and immediately clasps her in his arms. Obviously, eggs aren't on his mind. The relationship also has a hint of sadomasochism. Cleopatra laughingly protests, "Oh but you are strong. You're squeezing me to death." Hercules exults, "And you like it." "Oh, you're taking my breath away," she enthuses.

Freaks's racy content should not have been a detriment to its commercial success; *Dr. Jekyll and Mr. Hyde* had a considerable amount of that and it did well at the box office. The casting of dwarves was no problem; Harry Earles had appeared in both the silent and sound versions of *The Unholy Three*. Another dwarf, Angelo Rossitto, was already a veteran film performer and would continue to appear in movies for over half a century. The controversy was the casting of other sideshow "freaks."

The Siamese twins Daisy and Violet Hilton were joined at the buttocks. They were popular vaudeville performers, but they were treated as slaves by their guardian and manager. The twins had recently won a lawsuit against them; now in charge of their own lives, they voluntarily joined the *Freaks* cast. Jane Barnell, alternately billed as "Lady Olga," "Madame Olga," and "Princess Olga," was a bearded lady. Johnny Eck had no legs. Randian had neither legs nor hands. Several victims of microcephaly were also cast in *Freaks*.

These mentally-challenged people with abnormally-small craniums were billed in sideshows as "pinheads." One of them, called Schlitze, was a man who masqueraded as a woman in a dress, supposedly due to incontinence. These were just some of the physically-abnormal people who populated Browning's production.

The physically-normal people on the MGM lot were uneasy when they saw the "freaks." Producer Harry Rapf bemoaned, "People run out of the commissary and throw up!" One of the nauseated people was F. Scott Fitzgerald. The distinguished author was toiling as a screenwriter to help pay the bills for his wife's institutional care. He planned to have lunch at a table when the Hilton twins joined him. Fitzgerald turned green and left. In order to pacify the people who weren't working on *Freaks*, the human oddities were given their own lunch tables away from the commissary. The Earles siblings and the Hilton twins, however, were allowed to eat with the physically-normal people.

Browning's original cut of *Freaks* began with the sideshow performers frolicking by the lake and ended with the castrated Hercules singing in a high-pitched voice in the sideshow. But the preview was a disaster. Art director Merill Pye, who was there, later recalled that halfway through the screening, "a lot of people got up and ran out. They didn't walk out. They *ran* out." MGM, hoping that *Freaks* could be made more palatable for moviegoers, ordered Tod Browning to make revisions. Browning spent four days shooting retakes. Hercules's falsetto number was scissored out. In the released version, Hercules is last seen with a knife in his back, his ultimate fate a mystery. The director concocted a framing device of the carnival barker who explains to the patrons how Cleopatra became a "freak." He also added a sentimental coda of Hans and Frieda's reunion.

MGM might as well have not bothered making any changes to *Freaks*. Some critics spewed their vitriol about the film. *Harrison's Reports* complained, "Anyone who considers this entertainment, should be placed in the pathological ward in some hospital." John C. Moffit in the Kansas City *Star* fumed, "There is no excuse for this picture. It took a weak mind to produce it and it takes a strong stomach to look at it … In 'FREAKS' the movies make their great step toward national censorship. If they get it, they will have no one to blame but themselves."

Other critics expressed their misgivings, although they found merit in the film. John Mosher in *The New Yorker* considered *Freaks* "a little gem, but at the same time, a perverse one. There isn't anything wholesome about it ... Its morbidity lies beyond the boundaries of anything like dear, simple sex." Richard Watts, Jr. in the New York *Herald Tribune* contended, "It is obviously an unhealthy and generally disagreeable work, not only in its story and characterization, but also in its ... directorial touches. Mr. Browning can even make freaks more unpleasant than they would be ordinarily. Yet, in some strange way, the picture is not only exciting, but even occasionally touching." Most of the critics worried that *Freaks* would corrupt the morals of youthful patrons.

Some moviegoers actually enjoyed *Freaks*. It is likely they paid to see the physical abnormalities on the screen for the same reason they paid to see them in the sideshow—morbid curiosity. When it played for four days at the Court Street Theatre in Buffalo, New York, the box office gross was twice the average amount. Minneapolis' State Theatre prohibited children from seeing *Freaks*, but the film sent the take of the house a thousand dollars above average. Many more moviegoers, however, stayed away. The Midland Theatre in Kansas City tirelessly promoted *Freaks*, but it set a record for poor grosses. Perhaps the people in Kansas City took John C. Moffit's screed to heart. Some who did see *Freaks* were appalled. One patron wrote to *Photoplay*, "I didn't mind its gruesomeness so much, but its cheap vulgarity is something that left a bad taste in my mouth. I am not easily shocked and do not hold with rigid censor laws. What amazes me is its frightfully bad taste." Not surprisingly, *Freaks* got into trouble with the censors. The film did well in Los Angeles, but exhibitors there were forced to close it. Exhibitors in San Francisco and Atlanta didn't get a chance to show the film at all. *Freaks* was also banned from showings in Great Britain. On August 7, 1932, MGM pulled the film from distribution. It suffered a net loss of $164,000.

The strengthening of the Production Code didn't prevent Hollywood from exploiting physically-deformed people for shocks.

In 1944, Universal cast real-life acromegalic Rondo Hatton as the homicidal Hoxton Creeper in the Sherlock Holmes suspense film *The Pearl of Death*. Hatton, who had been a football hero at the University of Florida, developed acromegaly after he was gassed in France as a soldier in World War I. The disease enlarged his facial features, feet, hands, and back. *The Pearl of Death* did well at the box office, and Universal cast him in several chillers. Hatton's career ended with his death on February 2, 1946, brought on by his condition. Three of his films were released posthumously.

For many years, *Freaks* was not shown in mainstream cinemas. Exploitation impresario Dwain Esper took the film on the roadshow circuit and added a preachy prologue in order to assure the authorities the film had educational value. With the relaxation of censorship guidelines and the rise of the avant-garde film scene in the early 1960s, new screenings of *Freaks* appeared in respectable movie houses. Now critics praised Tod Browning's film, hailing it as an innovative and compassionate work of art. In 1962, it was shown at the Venice Film Festival, and in 1967, it was shown at the Museum of Modern Art in New York City. *Freaks* has been aired on television, and it is available on commercial home video.

Even today, *Freaks* remains disturbing viewing. The sight of the mutilated Cleopatra is the most gruesome one in pre-Code horror cinema. Legless, with one eye partially closed, and only capable of emitting squawks from her mouth, she is both revolting and pitiful. The tacked-on epilogue of Hans and Frieda's reunion cannot dispel the memory of the beauty transformed into a "freak." Cleopatra's fate is truly one that is worse than death.

Tod Browning gives the viewers mixed messages about the genuine "freaks." At first, he takes pains to establish them as cheerful and pleasant people, despite their infirmities. He shows us how they've dealt with their handicaps. For example, the legless Johnny Eck walks on his hands with ease, and the limbless Randian effortlessly rolls and lights a cigarette with his mouth. Browning also uses gentle humor to examine the inconveniences of the Hilton twins' romantic life; one of them marries a circus performer and he tries to adjust to living with a wife who is always attached to her sister. The birth of the bearded lady's hirsute baby is treated as a joyous event, just as if a physically-normal woman gave birth to a physically-normal baby.

After the "freaks" learn that Cleopatra is trying to poison Hans, Browning suddenly utilizes them for horrific effect. The director provides menacing shots of them spying on her. When the "freaks" perform their grisly revenge on Cleopatra and Hercules, Browning no longer depicts them as human beings but as monsters, creeping toward the terrified "normal" people in the thunderstorm. An especially-troubling shot is Randian inching toward Hercules with a knife between his teeth. Browning becomes insensitive and exploitive toward the "freaks;" he is as much a villain as Cleopatra and Hercules.

Jane Barnell was one "freak" who was unhappy with the film. After its release, her manager declared, "Miss Barnell thinks this picture was an insult to all freaks everywhere and is sorry she acted in it." Johnny Eck couldn't stand looking at himself on the screen: "It made me very self-conscious. Until then I never realized how horrible I look." But unlike Miss Barnell, he didn't regret making *Freaks* and considered Tod Browning a "prince."

Freaks may have appalled the public, but that didn't mean that macabre films were on the way out. Moviegoers enjoyed being scared as long as they knew the monsters who scared them were make believe. Two enterprising brothers, Edward and Victor Halperin, planned a new film with a bunch of different fanciful monsters, the zombies. Creating and leading these zombies would be the legendary screen Dracula Bela Lugosi. Already, the Hungarian actor was becoming identified with the horror genre.

WHITE ZOMBIE [1932]

Released on July 28, 1932; A United Artists Release of a Halperin Brothers Production; *Director:* **Victor Halperin;** *Producers:* **Edward and Victor Halperin;** *Story and Dialogue:* **Garrett Weston;** *Photographer:* **Arthur Martinelli;** *Editor:* **Harold MacLernon;** *Art Direction:* **Ralph Berger and Conrad Tritschler;** *Dialogue Director:* **Herbert Farjeon;** *Makeup:* **Jack P. Pierce and Carl Axcelle;** *Special Effects:* **Harold Anderson;** *Original Music:* **Guy Bevier Williams and Xavier Cugat;** *Musical Arrangements:* **Abe Meyer;** *Additional Music:* **Nathaniel Dett, Gaston Borch, Hugo Riesenfeld, Leo Kempenski, H. Herkan and H. Maurice Jacquet; 73 minutes.**

Cast: **Bela Lugosi (Murder Legendre), Madge Bellamy (Madeline Short), John Harron (Neil Parker), Joseph Cawthorn (Dr. Bruner), Robert Frazer (Charles Beaumont), Clarence Muse (Driver), Brandon Hurst (Silver), Dan Crimmins (Pierre), Frederick Peters (Chauvin) George Burr McAnnan (Von Gelder), John T. Prince (Latourr).**

SYNOPSIS: Charles Beaumont invites the engaged American couple Madeline Short and Neil Parker to his plantation in Haiti for their wedding. But Beaumont secretly desires Madeline, and he visits the sinister sugar mill owner and zombie master Murder Legendre for supernatural assistance. The fiend gives Beaumont a potion, and Beaumont surreptitiously gives it to Madeline. After the wedding, the bride suddenly drops dead and is buried. Legendre and Beaumont disinter Madeline's body, and she is revived as a zombie. Horrified over Madeline's catatonic state, Beaumont implores Legendre to return her to normal. The treacherous Legendre, who lusts for Madeline, slowly turns Beaumont into a zombie. Meanwhile, Neil discovers that Madeline's body is no longer in the tomb and seeks the aid of missionary Dr. Bruner, an expert on *zombie practices. The two go to Legendre's castle on a cliff to rescue Madeline and stop Legendre. Legendre orders his zombies to attack Neil and Bruner, but Bruner knocks the zombie master out, and the slaves, unable to think for themselves, walk off the cliff to their deaths. Legendre resumes consciousness, but Beaumont, who has regained some of his strength, kills him. When Legendre dies, Madeline is freed from her spell and is reunited with Neil.*

White Zombie was a milestone in horror cinema history—the first feature about the zombie legend. Indeed, the term *zombie*, originating in Haitian folklore and derived from the Bantu language, was new in the American English lexicon. William Seabrook made the word popular in a 1929 book *The Magic Island*. This work was purportedly an eyewitness account of voodoo ceremonies in Haiti. It wasn't a reliable account, but it sold well; most Americans were unfamiliar with Haitian folklore, and they were enthralled by the book's claims. *The Magic Island*'s success inspired a short-lived play, *Zombie*, staged in early 1932. When Edward and Victor Halperin concocted *White Zombie*, the play's author Kenneth Webb tried to sue the brothers for copyright infringement. The Halperins proved that the zombie legend had existed long before Webb was born—no individual could claim intellectual rights to this concept.

The film's title played on White Americans' xenophobia and racism; a Caucasian victimized by a "foreign" and "savage" magic. A catchline in *White Zombie*'s exhibitor pressbook proclaimed, "They [Whites] knew that this was taking place among the blacks, but when this fiend practiced it on a white girl—all hell broke loose." The voodoo master, however, was a Caucasian himself. The Hollywood studios didn't care about Black sensibilities—the civil rights movement didn't impact the country until the 1960s; they were uneasy about the concept of a Black person dominating a White person. Nevertheless, the Halperin brothers cast a "foreign" actor as the voodoo master, an otherworldly figure to contrast with the innocent American visitors who encounter him in Haiti. The Hungarian Bela Lugosi was cast as the voodoo master Murder Legendre, reminiscent of his earlier Dracula role.

Like Dracula, Legendre yearns for a delicate maiden who is engaged to a respectable young man. But this young man, Neil (John Harron), has to contend with another rival, Beaumont (Robert Frazer). *White Zombie*'s romantic intrigue is more tangled and suspenseful than *Dracula*'s. Beaumont desires the maiden Madeline (Madge Bellamy), but she has no interest. He seeks Legendre's help to win Madeline's love—Legendre has the power to *force* the woman to fall for Beaumont. Legendre makes Madeline Beaumont's love slave.

Madeline's somnambulistic state horrifies Beaumont. "I thought that beauty alone would satisfy," he laments. "But the soul is gone. I can't bear those empty, staring eyes." When Beaumont tells Legendre to free her from her trance, the treacherous voodoo master makes *him* a zombie. Legendre plans to possess Madeline himself.

The premise of a man manipulating a woman's mind to make her a docile inamorata had already been used in the previous year's borderline horror *Svengali*. As Tom Johnson points out in *Censored Screams: The British Ban on Hollywood Horror in the Thirties*, "This is pretty strong stuff, even for the pre-Code days, and one presumes that it was only in a horror-fantasy context that these perverted sexual dominations could have been permitted."

Unlike Svengali, however, Legendre has no carnal interest in his prey. He only wants to subjugate her to his will. Legendre is too cold and calculating to feel true passion. Lugosi looks dashing with a goatee in a black cloak and broad-brimmed hat, but he lacks Dracula's dark allure. Unlike the vampire, who commits atrocities to sustain himself, Legendre commits atrocities because he relishes them.

Nevertheless, the publicity department knew that sex was a marketable angle for *White Zombie*. No doubt they knew about the successful sensual ads for *Dracula*. *White Zombie*'s ads were likewise suggestive. One poster displayed Lugosi's staring eyes and clenched hands, and nothing else. The tagline was "WITH THESE ZOMBIE EYES he rendered her powerless WITH THIS ZOMBIE GRIP he made her perform his every desire!" Another poster had a similar tagline: "SHE WAS NOT ALIVE ... NOR DEAD ... Just a WHITE ZOMBIE Performing his every desire!" Depicted on this poster opposite Lugosi's demonic visage was an entranced

Madge Bellamy in a flimsy dressing gown, one breast exposed. An even more provocative ad displayed a startled Bellamy wearing nothing but a necklace and a bracelet.

Bellamy herself is demurely clothed throughout most of *White Zombie*, even in her zombie state. There is one scene where the audience sees her in bridal lingerie. Had the film been made after the Code was strengthened, the censors would have insisted that Bellamy would never be shown in her underwear, bridal or otherwise. But the filmmakers don't show her in scanties just to titillate viewers. While she waits for one of the maids to get her wedding dress, another maid opens the window. Suddenly, the audience hears voodoo drums. When the second maid tells Bellamy that the drumming drives away evil spirits, the alarmed bride-to-be gasps, "Close it! Close it!"

Madge recovers her composure, but the innocent American heroine, frightened by the alien sound of voodoo drumming, is a stark image of vulnerability. Dressed only in lingerie, she looks even more defenseless. What if these strange drummers saw her half naked? This scene, alas, plays on the miscegenation fears of White filmgoers. Later in the film, Neil articulates them. When he discovers his bride's body is missing from the tomb, Dr. Bruner speculates she may not be dead: "Well, surely you don't think she's alive in the hands of the natives!" Neil frets, "Oh no, better dead than that."

If *White Zombie* addresses miscegenation paranoia, the film also touches on White colonial oppression. At the time of its release, the predominantly-Black nation of Haiti was under American occupation. In 1915, the U.S. Marines invaded the country because American bankers complained Haiti owed them money. Martial law was proclaimed in Haiti, and the natives were subjected to forced labor. The Haitians resented the American occupation and clashed with the troops. Finally in 1934, American forces withdrew from the nation, and its sovereignty was restored.

Tony Williams, in his essay "*White Zombie:* Haitian Horror" in the magazine *Jump Cut*, points out, "... zombie slavery in the film ... represents a macabre version of the forced labor system which the U.S. inflicted on the Haitian population in 1918" and "Legendre represents a distorted embodiment of U.S. guilt feelings concerning the occupation." This symbolism is particularly evident in an early scene where Beaumont sees Legendre's zombies in the sugar mill.

These somnambulant souls in ragged clothes toil to provide sugar for their master's plantation, especially the zombies grinding the sugar. The grinders languidly push the wheels to activate the blades. One of the zombies stumbles into the blades, but the others continue with their work as if nothing has happened. Legendre boasts to Beaumont about his zombies' docility: "They work faithfully and they are not worried about long hours." He then advises him, "You could make good use of men like mine on your plantation."

It is unlikely the filmmakers intended this scene as a subtle critique of the American occupation of Haiti. But Black viewers and some liberal White viewers may have interpreted it this way. If *White Zombie* does address this subject, it then runs away from it. The film only focuses on Madeline's plight. At the film's end, she is freed from her spell. Legendre's zombie henchmen, deprived of a master, kill themselves. Presumably, the zombie laborers also kill themselves, but *White Zombie* never alerts the viewers about *their* fates. The native Haitians' predicament isn't as important as that of a visiting American woman. Whether or not the filmmakers knew it, they trivialized the Haitians' real-life plight.

White Zombie's publicists may not have been concerned about the Haitians, but they were concerned about offending filmgoers. No doubt they remembered the earlier shocker *Freaks*, how the film's exploitation of actual physical oddities appalled the public. One tagline assured patrons, "This Picture Will Scare You ... But It Will Be a Pleasant Scare! You'll Know Such Things Cannot Happen Yet You'll Be Thrilled by This Black Magic of Haiti!" Considering *White Zombie*'s commercial success, the patrons obviously found its chills entertaining, not repugnant.

White Zombie's horror is suggested and stylized; it has none of *Freaks*'s grisliness. The zombie's fatal accident in the sugar mill is not depicted; the shock derives from his sudden stumble into the blades and the other zombies' lack of reactions. When Neil shoots one of the zombies, we see a close-up of a bullet hole in his torso. The sight is frightening because no blood appears; this zombie is truly inhuman and indestructible. It is a fantastical scare like Legendre's sorcery; not a realistic scare.

Nevertheless, the industry trade publication *Harrison's Reports* deemed *White Zombie* "[n]ot suitable for children for Sunday showing." The writer opined, "The type of audiences that go in for horror pictures will enjoy it . . . As for other types, it is too gruesome to be entertaining for them. . . ."

Ironically, some critics found the film to be too inept to be frightening. Thornton Delehaney in the New York *Evening Post* contended, "Obviously designed to titillate the spinal column, the story strains and struggles to out-*Frankenstein Frankenstein,* and so earnest is it in its attempts to be thrilling that it overreaches the mark all along the line and resolves into an unintentional and often hilarious comedy." *Time* sniffed, "The acting of everybody in *White Zombie* suggest that there may be some grounds for believing in zombies."

Not all the critics pilloried *White Zombie*, but even if they did, the public would have probably ignored them. *Variety* reported that filmgoers definitely ignored the reviews at the Warner Theater in Pittsburgh, Pennsylvania: "Despite critical panning, horror film packing them, with ballyhoo [publicity] methods given most of the credit." Indeed, an industry trade ad boasted of the disparity between critical and audience responses: "When Their Noses Turned Up Business Turned Up Too!" But there was no consensus among cinema owners whether or not to permit children to see *White Zombie*.

The Warner Theater in Milwaukee, Wisconsin encouraged boys and girls to see the film. Indeed, the Milwaukee *Sentinel*'s Sunday funnies section for the week of August 29 had a "Lucky Buck" coupon for them. Any youngster who brought the coupon to the Warner could see *White Zombie* for free. But the United Artists Theater in San Francisco, California proclaimed in its ads, "Only Adults Can See It!" This provocative admonition enticed mature filmgoers, resulting in impressive ticket sales over the film's eighteen-day run. These two contrasting marketing ploys reveal that in 1932, when public morals were theoretically more rigorous, some exhibitors considered a specific film to be less offensive than others.

The strengthening of the Production Code did not prevent *White Zombie* from being reissued in the late 1930s. Indeed, the Code found nothing objectionable in the film to cut for rerelease. Future film historian George E. Turner, who attended a 1938 screening in Regina Theatre in Los Angeles, observed that his fellow filmgoers, far from being scared, found the film risible:

"Film acting had become more naturalistic in style during the ensuing six years ... *White Zombie*—with its declamatory speeches and ancient music cues—seemed ... outmoded ... Every line of dialogue drew howls and hoots from the rowdier members of the audience. Before long they were repeating Lugosi's lines loudly, exaggerating his Hungarian accent ... A later trip to the Regina proved futile; the same rubes were back, but by this time they had memorized Lugosi's lines and were reciting them in synch with the actor!"

Had *White Zombie* been released in 1938 instead of 1932, it likely would have been a box office failure. Universal would not have bothered making *Son of Frankenstein*. The horror genre would have remained dormant for a longer time. But *White Zombie* was a hit, encouraging Universal to produce more horror films. Paramount also planned new shockers, and other studios hopped on the terror bandwagon. One of these studios was Warner Brothers. Their new film would be the horror debut for two legendary thespians, Lionel Atwill and Fay Wray.

DOCTOR X (1932)

Released on August 3, 1932 by Warner Brothers; *Director:* **Michael Curtiz;** *Screenplay:* **Robert Tasker and Earl Baldwin,** *based on the play by Howard W. Comstock and Allen C. Miller; Photography in two-color Technicolor process:* **Ray Rennahan;** *Art Director:* **Anton Grot;** *Editor:* **George Amy;** *Mask Effects:* **Max Factor Co.;** *Vitaphone Orchestra Conductor:* **Leo F. Forbstein; 77 minutes.**

Cast: **Lionel Atwill (Dr. Xavier), Fay Wray (Joanne Xavier), Lee Tracy (Lee Taylor), Preston Foster (Dr. Wells), John Wray (Dr. Haines), Harry Beresford (Dr. Duke), Arthur Edmund Carewe (Dr. Rowitz), Leila Bennett (Mamie), Robert Warwick (Stevens), George Rosener (Otto), Willard Robertson (O'Halloran), Thomas Jackson (Editor), Harry Holman (Policeman), Mae Busch (The Madame), Tom Dugan (Sheriff).**

SYNOPSIS: *A series of "moon murders," eerie killings involving cannibalism that always take place during a full moon, have occurred in the vicinity of Dr. Xavier's medical academy. Dr. Xavier asks the police for permission to do his own investigation of the crimes, and they reluctantly give him forty-eight hours. In order to avoid publicity, Xavier tries to solve the mysteries at his residence, Cliff Manor. He devises an experiment on his suspects, all doctors at his academy, to determine which one is the murderer. But when this process is carried out, one of them is killed. Meanwhile, reporter Lee Taylor is snooping on the grounds. When Xavier devises another experiment, his daughter Joan volunteers to participate in it. During this process, the culprit is exposed—Dr. Wells. He has been using the victims to create synthetic flesh. Wells threatens Joan, but Taylor vanquishes him. Taylor and Joan fall in love and plan to get married.*

Doctor X is a quintessential pre-Code Warners product. Most of the film's action centers in the archetypical creepy mansion, a popular setting for earlier whodunits. Stock mystery characters like the creepy butler and the frightened maid populate this film. But *Doctor X*'s hero Lee Taylor is a wisecracking reporter, played by Lee Tracy. The actor had played Hildy Johnson in the original Broadway production of *The Front Page*, and he was typecast as a smart-alecky reporter in films. Taylor toils in the urban milieu, a common setting for the studio's gritty dramas. And *Doctor X* touches on the city's vices of drug peddling and prostitution. Indeed, one of the Moon Killer's victims is a dope fiend and another is a streetwalker.

Early in the film, Lee phones his boss about the Moon Killer from a brothel while eyeing the hookers. Lamar Trotti, assistant to Col. Jason Joy, advised producer Jack Warner that the reporter should phone from a speakeasy. Reynold Humphries, in *The Hollywood Horror Film 1931-1941: Madness in a Social Landscape*, notes, "Apparently a journalist entering an establishment forbidden by law caused the Hays Office [another name for the MPPDA] no qualms, though whether this indifference stemmed from a contempt for journalists or a belief that alcoholism is preferable to extramarital sex remains unclear." Warner obviously recognized Trotti's suggestion was absurd since he ignored it.

Doctor X was adapted from a Broadway play. Running briefly a year before the film's release, the play was a comedy mystery with an ordinary mortal killer. To capitalize on the new horror genre, Warners' screenwriters made the murderer a one-armed mad scientist who creates a synthetic appendage from his victims' flesh. The pivotal scene where Professor Wells (Preston Foster) charges the limb with electricity and attaches it to his stump is not only gruesome but perverse as well. As David J. Hogan points out in *Dark Romance: Sexuality in the Horror Film*, he "fits it to his stump with all the glee of an impotent man trying out a new sex organ."

This disturbing sequence rattled both critics and filmgoers. *Harrison's Reports* called it "the most horrible thing seen in any horror picture, even worse than the transformation scene in *Dr. Jekyll and Mr. Hyde.*" Reviewers observed that people would scream when Professor Wells revealed his synthetic arm. But the scene didn't alienate the public the way the real-life human oddities did in *Freaks*; *Doctor X* made a profit. Unlike the "freaks," the electrically-charged appendage was science fiction.

Since *Doctor X* was a mystery, the film didn't expose Wells as the killer until the climax. Like all mysteries, this film was chock-full of red herrings. In his horror debut, Lionel Atwill as Dr. Xavier imbues his lines with sinister insinuations, a mad gleam frequently in his eyes. So charismatically creepy is he, more so than the actual villain Foster, one understands why Atwill quickly became typecast as a bogeyman. Even though his character commits no crimes in the picture, he is an unnerving presence. One wonders, even at the end, if the venerable doctor harbors any dark secrets.

One example will suffice. Xavier assigns his servants to reenact the Moon Killer's latest murder in front of the suspected scientists. He thinks one of the scientists, tormented by anxiety, will expose himself as the murderer. When the nervous maid Mamie (Leila Bennett) asks the doctor what part she will play, he replies, "The scrubwoman of course. The one who was murdered last night." Atwill, grinning, stresses the word *murdered*. When Mamie asks him why the butler Otto (George Rosener) isn't playing the victim, Xavier explains, "Otto has his own part, that of the killer." Atwill salivates over the word *killer*, his tone suggesting both sadism and perversity. Nearly a year later, Atwill would brazenly exhibit these depravities in *Murders in the Zoo*.

Xavier isn't the only suspect in *Doctor X* who seems depraved. Otto, who enjoys harassing Mamie, gooses her. Professor Haines (John Wray) conceals a magazine of French erotica in his scientific tome. Dr. Xavier naively tells the detectives, "He's inclined to be attentive to my daughter so I see a lot of him." Later in the film, when Taylor and Xavier's daughter Joanne (Fay Wray) fall in love on the beach, Haines glares at them. Perhaps he is jealous. It is also possible that he suspects that *Lee* is the Moon Killer.

Warner's originally intended Haines's desire for Joanne to be more obvious. A segment was filmed where the professor tries to entice her with Japanese pornography. Despite her protests, he opens the book and pushes it at her, drooling, "The drawings are a little naughty...." But then Dr. Xavier stops him and scolds Haines;

it isn't the first time the professor has violated sexual decorum. Haines sighs that Xavier still doesn't understand him. The scene was cut before release. It may have been cut not because the studio feared offending moviegoers but to improve the film's pacing. Even the romantic fadeout between Lee and Joanne at the film's end is kinky. Throughout the film, the reporter sports a joy buzzer ring, using it both intentionally and unintentionally on people. Lee forgets to take off the buzzer before he embraces Xavier's daughter. She enjoys the sensation, cooing, "Ooh, Mr. Taylor!"

If the sexual innuendo in *Doctor X* is strong, the film's violence is not. When Dr. Xavier examines the scrubwoman's corpse, he describes the killer's handiwork to the police: "You will notice how deeply the thumbs are embedded in the sternocleidomastoid... It's peculiar that this left deltoid muscle should be missing... It wasn't torn. This is cannibalism." The body per se, though, is not displayed; Xavier's explanation is sufficiently gruesome.

When the Moon Killer slays Dr. Rowitz (Arthur Edmund Carewe) during the reenactment of the scrubwoman's murder, the audience sees the scientist's distorted face but not the murderer. Why don't viewers see the Moon Killer's criminal act? The other scientists don't see it either. Dr. Xavier, hearing the scream, thinks Rowitz is panicked by the staging of the scrubwoman's death, betraying his guilt.

When Dr. Xavier realizes that Dr. Rowitz has been killed, he notes that he has been stabbed in the base of the brain. In a close-up of the corpse's face, there is a tiny red gash behind the right ear, nothing gorier. The actual murderer, Professor Wells, appears, claiming the Moon Killer struck him. He only has a small gash on his left forehead. Of course, this could simply be makeup to fool the other scientists. Wells doesn't wish to injure himself seriously; he wants future victims. Later, Dr. Haines examines Rowtiz's corpse. He begins to describe to Dr. Xavier the cadaver's appearance. Xavier interrupts Haines with "I know." The filmmakers only insinuate that the body has been gnawed at. John Wray's rattled performance is enough to inform audiences about the unspeakable.

The climactic fight between the Moon Killer and Lee Taylor is bloodless. Lee vanquishes the maniac with a lamp, engulfing him in flames. When the reporter pushes Wells through the window, director Michael Curtiz uses a long shot of the murderer's flaming body falling into the ocean. The dark lighting (it is night) further obscures the charred body's details. Had Wells' death been more graphically shown, the sight would have been artlessly repulsive rather than imaginatively stylish.

Despite the mild violence, *Doctor X* is an indisputably macabre film. But Warner Brothers' publicists, doubtlessly remembering the recent failure of *Freaks*, did not want to stress the film's horror aspect. "Sell its importance," the film's pressbook advised exhibitors, "its bigness—its novelty—its combination of mystery-thrills, love and comedy—its splendid technicolor effect. AVOID any suggestion of horror or shock. The picture contains more laughs and more romance than any mystery thriller ever made. It is important to get this over in your promotion." Among *Doctor X*'s catchlines were "The Most Mystifying Mystery in Years" and "It's the Miracle Film of 1932."

The brochure did not evade sex as a selling point. Indeed, the brochure was tailored to excite the theater owners. As *Film Daily* reported, ". . . the first page features a full-length figure of a very attractive blonde calling on the exhib with a cheery 'Good Morning! I'm here to help you sell 'Doctor X' as the blonde is only attired in a brassiere and a pair of panties.......you can well imagine that the tired and worried exhib is gonna perk up and give attention to this seductive Pressbook Saleslady...' Throughout the pressbook, the lady was pictured in a variety of provocative poses offering tips on how to promote *Doctor X*. The last page featured her tipping her hat and smilingly saying, "Call again, baby! We'll be glad to see you any time."

Despite its insistence on sidestepping the film's horror angle, the pressbook was not above using scare tactics to lure box office patrons. It suggested to exhibitors to make "MYSTERY PHONE CALLS:" "Use the phone in your 'Doctor X' exploitations, calling up as many people as possible every day before and during your showing. Have a man with a mysterious voice, corresponding to that of 'The Shadow' on the radio, tell the people who answer the phone—'You have an appointment with Doctor X—Do not slip up—he will be waiting—Remember because I do not forget—Ha! Ha! Ha! (dirty laugh)—The Phantom.'"

One exhibitor used a unique scare tactic to promote *Doctor X* at his theater. Max Melincoff of the Palace Theatre in Lawrence, Massachusetts persuaded a local pharmacy to devise a fake prescription. Displayed in a huge blow-up in a window at the Palace, the prescription read: "Doctor X, Palace Theatre Bldg., Lawrence, Mass. Office Hours 1 to 11 P.M. Continuous Daily. Patient's Name....... Address.......Lawrence. 1 Aspirin Tablet for nervous condition. This prescription will be filled without charge by (Druggist's name and address). Doctor X.......M.D. You Will Need This After Seeing 'Doctor X.'" Meanwhile, in Lexington, Kentucky, ticket buyers at the Ben Ali could not miss a bannered vehicle outside the theater. The banner stated: "This Ambulance Is to Carry Patrons Home From the Ben Ali Who Can't Stand the Excitement of Seeing Doctor X."

Dick Lashley, manager of the Carolina Theatre in Greenville, South Carolina, posted an advertisement offering five dollars to any woman who could sit alone through a special evening screening of *Doctor X*. This gimmick reflects Depression-era society's unenlightened attitudes toward women. According to *Motion Picture Herald*, more than fifteen hundred ladies applied for the job eight hours after the ad appeared. Five dollars was a substantial amount of money in 1932, especially since the country was in an economic crisis. The woman chosen to see *Doctor X* earned her money. She told the local press about her film-going experience, which in turn garnered more publicity for *Doctor X*.

Both men and women enjoyed being frightened. One box office patron in Chicago, Esther Anderson, was quoted in *The New Movie Magazine*: "If Hollywood doesn't stop scaring us all to death, the future film audience will be strapped in straitjackets soon. But who doesn't appreciate a spooky thrill? No matter how it scares you, you like it." Esther also encouraged the film producers to "[g]ive us more bogy-man pictures . . . and we'll spend all our money to go and get a good scare. The more I see the more I want!" Ironically, Chicago's censor board was the only one in America to insist on a cut in *Doctor X* before screening it for the public. According to *Film*

Daily, the censor board wanted one word eliminated, but the paper didn't explain what the word was. Presumably, the writer was worried that readers, like Chicago's censor board, would be offended.

Warner Brothers didn't have to worry about offended patrons. Encouraged by *Doctor X*'s success, the studio planned another Technicolor shocker directed by Michael Curtiz with Lionel Atwill and Fay Wray. This film, *Mystery of the Wax Museum*, would hit theaters in early 1933. Just a month after *Doctor X*'s release, RKO Radio would present its first horror film. Once again, Fay Wray would be the potential female victim.

THE MOST DANGEROUS GAME [1932]

Released September 16, 1932; RKO Radio Pictures, Inc.; Directors: **Ernest B. Schoedsack and Irving Pichel;** *Producers:* **Merian C. Cooper and Ernest B. Schoedsack;** *Executive Producer:* **David O. Selznick;** *Screenplay:* **James A. Creelman;** *Based on the short story by Richard Connell; Cinematography:* **Henry Gerrard;** *Art Director:* **Carroll Clark;** *Editor:* **Archie S. Marshek;** *Music:* **Max Steiner;** *Makeup Department:* **Wally Westmore;** *Special Effects:* **Harry Redmond, Jr; 63 minutes.**

Cast: **Joel McCrea (Bob Rainsford), Fay Wray (Eve Trowbridge), Robert Armstrong (Martin Trowbridge), Leslie Banks (Count Zaroff), Hale Hamilton (Bill Woodman), Noble Johnson (Ivan), Steve Clemento (Tartar), Dutch Hendrian (Scar-face), William B. Davidson (Captain), Landers Stevens (Doc), James Flavin (First Mate).**

SYNOPSIS: *A yacht sailing through shark-infested channels strikes a coral reef and sinks. The only surviving passenger is big game hunter Bob Rainsford, who swims to the shore of an island. There he meets Count Zaroff, who owns a fortress, and his guests, siblings Eve and Martin Trowbridge, who survived an earlier shipwreck. Zaroff, a refugee from Bolshevik Russia, is himself a big game hunter. Unlike Bob, who hunts animals, Zaroff hunts people. After Martin becomes Zaroff's latest quarry, the Count decides to hunt down Bob. Zaroff tells his unwilling prey that if he kills him before 4 AM, he will claim Eve as his trophy. Bob can have Eve if he outwits the Count. Eve, who is enraged at Zaroff for killing her brother, joins Bob on the lam. Together, they trek through the forest on the island, evading Zaroff's arrows. But Zaroff catches up with Bob and in the subsequent struggle, Bob falls off the cliff into the ocean. The Count brings Eve back to his fortress. To Zaroff's shock, Bob shows up there. The men engage in another battle, but Bob kills Zaroff and his henchmen and escapes with Eve from the island.*

Richard Connell's original narrative "The Most Dangerous Game," which was published in the magazine *Collier's* in 1924, is an intriguing but slender scenario. Its brevity was necessary for a short story but not for a feature film. In order to embellish Connell's plot, screenwriter James A. Creelman not only prolonged the suspense and beefed up the climax, but he added a spicy element missing from the original story—sex. In Connell's tale, Zaroff hunts men to prove his mental superiority over them. In the film adaptation, Zaroff (Leslie Banks) hunts men to satiate his carnal passions. Producer Merian C. Cooper explained the villain's twisted motivation: "He cannot love until he has known the thrill of the hunt with a human being as his prey. Such an atavistic creature is the man who by his savage instincts dominates the most dangerous game."

Zaroff does not mince words about this perversity. He informs his guests on his island, "You know the saying of the Ugandi chieftains, 'Hunt first the enemy, then the woman.' It is the natural instinct. What is woman . . . until the blood is quickened by the kill?" He gets more excited as he continues his speech: "One passion builds upon another. Kill! Then love. When you have known that you will have known ecstasy."

Such provocative dialogue would have been forbidden in the post-Code era. Leslie Banks gives his lines the necessary intensity. But if Lionel Atwill had played Zaroff, he would have seasoned the dialogue with insinuations of dirty-minded glee. He played a similar role of a wealthy sportsman who is aroused by killing in *Murders in the Zoo*. Atwill in *Murders in the Zoo* is a believable sex murderer; Banks in *The Most Dangerous Game* is, by contrast, an ordinary murderer.

Richard Connell's original story has no female characters. The screenwriter's invention of the character of Eve Trowbridge, played by Fay Wray, was meant to attract female box office patrons. *Variety*'s "Woman's Angle" columnist wasn't impressed: "Though charged with sympathy for its attractive victims, [the] plot is too fantastic and unpleasant to count on strong feminine support."

The character of Eve was also intended to provide sex appeal for male box office patrons. The gorgeous Wray scampers through the jungle in a slinky, low-cut gown that gets tattered, revealing more of her womanly attributes. Yet while *Most Dangerous Game* emphasizes the actress' pulchritude, it also stresses her innocence. Significantly, her name is Eve, the first woman according to the Old Testament. The film strongly implies that Count Zaroff threatens her virtue; he intends to bed her if he kills Bob Rainsford (Joel McCrea). Wray's ethereal beauty and genteel demeanor make her character believably angelic and vulnerable.

Merian C. Cooper contended, "Woman has retained, fortunately, the fighting, dominant blood of the savage. She would have perished as a distinctive individual long ago had it not been for her savage strain which has always given her the impetus of fighting for her rights. This quality can be found in the most fragile of women. For a long time, I always thought that 'the most dangerous' game naturally would be one in which a woman was involved." In the film, Wray's character Eve is not a formidable tigress. She doesn't devise any plans to outwit Zaroff in the jungle, but only goes along with Bob's plans. She also fails to elude Zaroff's clutches. But she insists on accompanying Bob on his travails in the jungle. Although captured by Zaroff, she escapes along with Bob. Eve may not be a warrior, but she is a survivor.

Fay Wray isn't the only titillating spectacle in *The Most Dangerous Game*. Zaroff's castle has a few salacious set design pieces. The door knocker is in the shape of a shirtless, bestial looking man holding an unconscious, scantily-clad woman in his arms. When Bob Rainsford ascends the staircase inside the castle, he notices a painting on the wall of a satyr clutching another unconscious, scantily-clad woman in his arms. Both artworks symbolize Zaroff's view of the female as a trophy to be possessed and shielded from others. The painting also plays on White Americans' paranoia about miscegenation: the satyr is dark skinned and the woman is fair.

Most Dangerous Game's shocks are lurid, befitting a pre-Code film. When a shark devours one of Rainsford's shipmates early in the film, the filmmakers depict the big fish with blood spewing from its mouth. Had the film been made in color, the censors likely would have stopped the filmmakers from showing the blood. Later in Zaroff's castle, one of the gruesome relics of the Count's huntings is displayed, a severed head floating in a jar of embalming fluid. Ernest Schoedsack, determined to make this grotesque object look convincing to moviegoers, actually went to a morgue to learn how human heads were preserved!

The Most Dangerous Game originally had scenes where Zaroff shows Rainsford more remains of his victims; these were cut before release. The demented sportsman exhibits a row of human heads and comments, "Stupid sailors—a thoroughbred dog is worth the lot of them!" He displays three mounted cadavers, a man and two hounds. Zaroff explains that the man "killed my two best dogs—in fact, the ones you see here with him. That's why I rarely use the brutes. Wound a man and they'll pull him down before you've a chance to make the kill yourself." The Count shows off another corpse pinned to a post by an arrow: "The foolish fellow tried to run through the swamps ... We preserved him just as he died, as an object lesson, you might say."

The bloodshed is restrained by today's standards, but it must have rattled Depression-era filmgoers. When Zaroff's henchman Ivan (Noble Johnson) is fatally impaled in Rainsford's makeshift trap, there is a close-up of blood trickling down one of his hands. In the climactic battle between the hero and the villain, Rainsford bloodies the left side of Zaroff's face. Not all of the film's violence is explicit. The corpse of Zaroff's victim Martin Trowbridge is never shown. Rainsford briefly lifts up the blanket to identify him and his appalled expression sufficiently conveys the horror of Martin's death.

Throughout the film, Zaroff sports a scar on the right side of his face, the result of a scuffle with a Cape buffalo in Africa. Leslie Banks didn't actually have that scar, but his left face was paralyzed, the result of a combat injury during World War I. World War I is not touched on in *The Most Dangerous Game*, but the Bolshevik Revolution in Russia, resulting from the country's disastrous handling of the conflict, is. As in Connell's short story, Zaroff is a refugee from Communist Russia. He tells Rainsford he was able to flee his native country "with most of my fortune."

Brought up as a privileged aristocrat, Zaroff believes that Divine Providence determines every person's social status. He avers, "God made some men poets. Some He made kings, some beggars. Me He made a hunter!" This helps explain Zaroff's remorseless manipulation of humans as prey. In Zarrow's twisted view, he hunts because God wills it. Moviegoers burdened by worries about their economic situation must have relished seeing this arrogant patrician pay for his hubris. Although most of *The Most Dangerous Game* takes place on a far away island, the film has a line of dialogue commenting on the Great Depression. When Zaroff, in talking about his passion of hunting, tells of his frustration finding worthy game in the Amazon, Martin (Robert Armstrong) remarks, "Well conditions are bad everywhere these days."

The Most Dangerous Game, unlike the original short story, confronts the ethical issue of hunting, be it people or animals. Early in the film, a passenger named Doc (Landers Stevens) tells the other ship passengers, including Rainsford, "I was thinking about the inconsistency of civilization. The beast of the jungle killing just for his existence is called savage. The man, killing just for sport, is called civilized ... It's a bit contradictory, isn't it?"

Rainsford, an enthusiastic hunter, himself, becomes defensive. He talks about his stalking of a tiger: "There never was a time when he couldn't have gotten away. He didn't want to. He got interested in hunting me. He didn't hate me for stalking him any more than I hated him for trying to charge me. As a matter of fact, we admired each other."

Doc continues to press the issue, asking Rainsford if he would change places with the tiger. Rainsford answers, "Well that's something I'll never have to decide. This world's divided into two kinds of people—the hunter and the hunted. Luckily, I'm a hunter. Nothing can ever change that." Just then, the ship crashes and this disaster ultimately results in Rainsford becoming the hunted. When he and Eve climb up a tree to escape Zaroff's hounds, Rainsford has an epiphany: "Those animals I cornered—now I know how they felt." Even though he survives Zaroff's hunt, he will never be the same.

In James Creelman's original script, Zaroff used leopards. Schoedsack later remembered, "He decided it would be more scary if Zaroff used hunting *leopards* instead of dogs. I reluctantly hired a leopard and its trainer from the Selig Zoo, and the cat immediately ran away on the jungle set. People were climbing to the rafters and we spent hours rounding him up." Because of this mishap, twenty Great Danes were used instead of leopards. Five of the dogs had been specially trained by the Hollywood Dog Training School.

Schoedsack said, "Some of . . . [the dogs] . . . belonged to Harold Lloyd and he didn't appreciate our blacking them up to make them look fiercer. Once, when we were working on the Fog Hollow set, Leslie came bounding out of the fog, clutching his rear end, and told us, 'I say, one of those dogs bit me!' The lady from the training school said, 'Oh no, it's impossible! None of those dogs would do that!' Leslie said, 'Well, perhaps it was a cameraman, but something bit me in the ass.' He was bleeding and had to have first aid and stitches." Banks must have been grateful he didn't have to work with leopards; they weren't domesticated like Great Danes were, and one of those big cats might have killed him.

Film editor Archie Marshek was pleased with *The Most Dangerous Game*: "I knew the picture was going to be a classic as soon as I'd seen a few of the dailies." But he also recalled, "At the preview there were two places where a lot of people walked out. One was when they saw a head floating in a jar, and the other was when McCrea broke a man's back." Box office patrons' reactions to the released film seemed to be mixed. Bert Silver of the Silver Family Theatre in Greenville, Michigan wrote to *The Motion Picture Herald*, "It would be impossible to make a more horrifying picture. Some liked it, some not, but if you want thrills this has 'em."

The Motion Picture Herald warned its readers, "It's entirely an adult picture, far too strong for children." *Modern Screen* advised its readers to "see it yourself before deciding to take the children." Reviewers' evaluations of *Most Dangerous Game*'s shocks varied. Some of them felt the film wasn't believably scary. Norbert Lusk in *Picture Play Magazine* opined, "Like many horror pictures, this is too determined. Consequently it falls short the mark and becomes merely fantastic, holding interest on the score of what the players will be up to next rather than any cumulative suspense or mounting thrill." Others believed the film effectively handled the horror aspects. George Blaidsell wrote in *The International Photographer*, "The story . . . is out of the ordinary, much. It is weird and shivery, plenty. Yet also somewhat out of the usual order in these creepy yarns the tale is entirely logical and imposes no strain on the credulity." Evidently, many box office patrons were satisfied with *The Most Dangerous Game*; the film made a profit for RKO.

Universal was determined to make money with a new shocker reuniting *Frankenstein*'s director James Whale and actor Boris Karloff. The studio intended to cast Karloff as a grotesque brute similar to Frankenstein's Monster. Once again, Jack Pierce provided gruesome makeup for the English actor. But James Whale had no intention of showcasing Karloff in another mad scientist film. Instead, the director planned to use the actor as an ensemble player in a creepy mansion thriller. This movie, *The Old Dark House*, would not be a run-of-the-mill thriller but an irreverent entertainment mixing horror and humor.

THE OLD DARK HOUSE [1932]

Released October 20, 1932; A Universal Picture; Director: **James Whale;** *Producer:* **Carl Laemmle, Jr.;** *Associate Producer:* **E.M. Asher;** *Screenplay:* **Benn W. Levy;** *Based on the novel* **Benighted** *by J.B. Priestley; Additional dialogue:* **R.C. Sherriff;** *Photography:* **Arthur Edeson;** *Art Director:* **Charles D. Hall;** *Editor:* **Clarence Kolster;** *Music:* **David Broekman;** *Makeup:* **Jack P. Pierce; 71 minutes.**

Cast: **Boris Karloff (Morgan), Melvyn Douglas (Roger Penderel), Gloria Stuart (Margaret Waverton), Charles Laughton (Sir William Porterhouse), Lillian Bond (Gladys DuCane), Ernest Thesiger (Horace Femm), Eva Moore (Rebecca Femm), Raymond Massey (Philip Waverton), Brember Wills (Saul Femm),Elspeth Dudgeon [billed as John Dudgeon] (Sir Roderick Femm).**

SYNOPSIS: On a stormy night in Wales, Philip Waverton, his wife Margaret, and their friend Roger Penderel seek refuge in a forbidding house off the road. They meet the strange residents—Horace Femm, his fanatical sister Rebecca, and their brutish butler Morgan. Later on more visitors find shelter there—widowed businessman Sir William Porterhouse and his companion Gladys DuCane. Roger and Gladys fall in love, and when they tell Porterhouse they plan to get married, he gives them his blessing. Philip and Margaret meet the bedridden patriarch Sir Roderick Femm. He warns them that locked in the house is another Femm, the pyromaniac Saul. Morgan hits the bottle which makes him violent, and he releases Saul. Saul tries to set fire to the house, but Roger stops him. They battle, resulting in Saul's death. The following morning, the storm has ended, the visitors leave, and Horace and Rebecca carry on as if nothing has happened.

When the English writer J.B. Priestley published *Benighted* in 1927, he didn't intend his novel to be a mere haunted-house shocker. It was meant to be an allegory about post–World War I disillusionment in his native Britain. In his words, it was "an attempt to transmute the thriller into symbolical fiction with some psychological depth." Priestley's grotesques in the old house where the visitors stay on a rainy night were meant to represent "various forms of post-war pessimism pretending to be real people." When Harpers published his book in the United States, it changed the title. In order to play up its horror aspects and avoid, in the writer's words, "any pretensions the book might have had to be a psychological or philosophical novel," the American publisher changed the title to *The Old Dark House.*

In adapting Priestley's book to the screen, Carl Laemmle, Jr. also wanted to stress its horror aspects. He envisioned it as a lucrative reteaming of *Frankenstein*'s director James Whale and actor Boris Karloff. Laemmle was especially interested in building up Karloff's marquee value. For the first time in his film career, the English actor would receive first billing. This credit was misleading, since Karloff's character of the savage butler Morgan is a supporting role. In fact, *The Old Dark House* is an ensemble piece. Ernest Thesiger (in his American film debut) as the acerbic yet timorous Horace Femm, and Melvyn Douglas as the cynical Roger Penderel, who is revitalized by love, more or less dominate on the screen. But *The Old Dark House*'s real star is director James Whale.

Tom Weaver, Michael Brunas, and John Brunas speculate in *Universal Horrors,* "The suggestion of a film version of *Benighted* ... was probably Whale's ... The book probably struck an emotional cord with the director who saw past the melodramatic plot to Priestley's trenching underlying theme of modernism encroaching on post-war Britain...." The British director may have particularly identified with Roger Penderel, a haunted World War I veteran. Whale had fought in the war and was imprisoned in a German POW camp. His first directorial film, *Journey's End* (1930), dramatized the agonies of trench warfare. His second project, *Waterloo Bridge* (1931), took place during the war; its heroine, Myra (Mae Clarke), was killed by a bomb from an air raid.

Nevertheless, James must have recognized that Universal wasn't interested in the book's philosophical undertones. *Universal Horrors*'s authors comment, "One could well imagine Whale ... pitching the project to Universal as a *Cat and the Canary*-style chiller while downplaying its inherent social subtext." Whale had seen and enjoyed Universal's silent mystery. He particularly liked the film's mixture of scares and laughs. The director would use this approach for *The Old Dark House*. Charles D. Hall, who was art director for *The Cat and the Canary*, would be the art director for Whale's film.

The author's commentary on hierarchy must have resonated with Whale. Born and raised in a working class environment, he painstakingly learned the mannerisms of the sophisticated upper class to succeed in British society and masquerade as the aristocrat he never was. But like the self-made Porterhouse, he resented people who actually *were* raised in wealth and privilege. R.C. Sherriff, who provided additional dialogue for *The Old Dark House*, once introduced Whale to some upper-class acquaintances. The director treated them with icy scorn, never able to forget the stigma of his lowly origins.

Priestley uses the characters of Rebecca and Saul Femm to skewer religious fanaticism. Whale augments the author's assaults. Bryan Senn points out in *Golden Horrors*, "Through Rebecca Femm, Whale exposes the traps of dogma and hypocrisy. Rebecca has become a sour, embittered woman who clings to her rituals yet has dispensed with the feeling behind them. She has twisted religion to suit her own dour personality."

While Margaret (Gloria Stuart) takes off her wet clothes and puts on an evening gown in a bedroom, Rebecca (Eva Moore) harangues her about the sins of vanity and "fleshly love." She then carefully arranges her hair in a mirror just before she leaves the room, hinting at Whale's dark humor, which Priestley's novel lacks. At dinner, Rebecca scolds Horace for not saying grace. But then she prays in a perfunctory rush.

In Priestley's book, Saul Femm's religious mania is vague and incoherent. In the film, Saul's zeal is more focused, though no less deranged. The lunatic (Brember Wills) identifies with his namesake, the tormented King in the Old Testament. Clutching a knife, he tells Penderel, "Saul *loved* David. But Saul was afraid of David because the Lord was with him and was departed from Saul ... And there was a javelin in Saul's hand and Saul *cast* the javelin." Thrusting the knife on to the table in front of Penderel, he goes on, "And he said, 'I will smite David even to the wall with it.'" He throws the knife at the wall, barely missing Penderel. *The Old Dark House* also targets Horace's professed atheism. He derides Rebecca's praying rituals as "strange tribal habits." Horace sardonically tells the visitors, "The beef will seem less tough when she has invoked a blessing upon it." But his cynical airs evaporate when he thinks his life is threatened.

When Philip Waverton (Raymond Massey) and Penderel tell him they need to stay at the Femms' house because the roads are flooded, Horace is so startled that he drops a bowl from his hands, shattering it on the floor. "We're trapped! We're trapped! We've got to go! You hear? We've got to go!" he wails to Rebecca. She smugly replies, "You don't believe in God and yet you're afraid to die!" Later, it is revealed that Horace is wanted by the police; the reason is never specified. But one can understand why Horace is terrified. At the film's end, when the storm has ended, Horace resumes his cynical demeanor. But when he tells the visitors, "The floods have subsided considerably," there is more than a hint of relief in his eyes. And the law doesn't catch up with him.

Benighted was published in the late 1920s during a period of relative prosperity. *The Old Dark House* was released during the Great Depression. Boris Karloff biographer Scott Allen Nollen points out that the film evokes the atmosphere of this harsh period. Consider the situation of Gladys DuCane (Lillian Bond), Sir William Porterhouse's companion. She says she's not a very good chorus girl. "If I were better at my job," she admits to the wealthy man, "I wouldn't be weekending with you." After an awkward pause, Gladys tries to amend this remark: "No I take that back. I probably would. You're nice enough." There is no suggestion of any sexual relations between Gladys and Porterhouse. She is simply a friend to help alleviate the widower's gloom. "He likes people to think he's ever so gay," she later tells Penderel when they are alone together. "You see, for all his money he's a bit lonely." "I think he's in love with that dead wife still," Roger says. When Gladys tells Porterhouse she's fallen in love with Roger, he magnanimously accepts this. But when he learns that Penderel isn't rich, he tells her, "I think you're a lunatic." A lot of 1932 filmgoers would have agreed.

When Gloria Stuart changes her clothes, the audience sees her in her undergarments. But this is not a gratuitous cheesecake bit. In the scene, Rebecca rants about hellfire and damnation while Margaret is changing her clothes. Mrs. Waverton is visibly uneasy; the audience knows she wants the harridan to leave. Rebecca taunts her: "You think of nothing but your long, straight legs and your white body—and how to please your man." Looking at Margaret in her evening dress, the old woman declares, "That's fine stuff—but it'll rot!" Poking at Margaret's bosom, she says, "That's finer stuff, still—but it'll rot, too, in time!" Margaret cries, "Don't! How dare you!" After Rebecca leaves, she touches her own bosom, looking disturbed. Does she feel violated because of Rebecca? Or does she wonder if she really is damned because of her modern lifestyle?

Gloria Stuart later recalled, "James had me change into a Jean Harlow style, bias-cut, pale pink velvet gown with spaghetti straps and earrings and pearls. And I said, 'Why me, James? Nobody else is changing; why am I changing?' He said, 'Because Boris is going to chase you up and down the corridors, up and down the stairs, and I want you to appear as a white flame...' It was strictly a matter of camera and style—there was no legitimate reason for me being in that dress. Lillian Bond didn't have to change, and she came in very wet. But Karloff didn't chase her."

In the film, Morgan doesn't seem very interested in Gladys. When she goes outside for an intimate conversation with Roger in the car, the butler sees her through the window. He smashes his fist through the pane, scaring her away. But instead of pursuing her, Morgan resumes his drinking. Later, when Gladys tries to get past him to see the injured Roger, he pushes her to the floor. Morgan grabs at Margaret, but she dissuades him when she tells him that Saul is also hurt. (In fact, Saul is dead). The brutish Morgan inexplicably has a soft spot for the homicidal Saul.

Morgan's lust for Margaret isn't the greatest threat; it's Saul's pyromania. James Whale artfully builds up Saul's menace with hints such as eerie laughter from behind a locked door. The director confounds expectations with Saul's first appearance. A slight, frail-looking old man, he seems gentle and vulnerable. "Don't let them put me back. I'm not mad," he pleads to Roger. But when Penderel turns away, the director employs a close-up of Saul looking crafty, his lip curled and one eyebrow raised. Sitting at a table with Roger, Saul is initially calm. But as he talks about flames and Saul in the Bible, he becomes more excited. All semblance of rationality disappears when he tries to knife Penderel and attempts to burn the house down. Whale uses characterization and dialogue, rather than sex and gruesomeness, for *The Old Dark House*'s strongest shocks.

In *Benighted*, Roger Penderel perishes in his climactic battle with Saul. An early script had Roger die, but by the time of shooting, Universal decided that like Henry Frankenstein, he should be spared. *The Old Dark House* ends with Roger proposing to Gladys. But Whale's irreverent humor prevails in this scene; Porterhouse is sleeping and his snoring is quite audible.

When Jason Joy viewed a preview of *The Old Dark House*, he found nothing objectionable. Indeed, he was delighted with it. He wrote to Carl Laemmle Jr., "Mr. Whale, as well as members of the cast, are to be congratulated on the excellence of their work . . . [I] enjoyed the picture thoroughly and wish you every success with it."

Universal's publicity department played up *The Old Dark House*'s horror aspects. An advertisement in the *New York Times* proclaimed, "Ten souls storm-bound in a house accursed! Murderous maniac—drink-mad monster—harpy—coward—fire fiend. Two beautiful women to be protected—three decent men not enough!" The ad's last line reveals American society's attitude toward women at the time. In Universal's mystery *The Secret of the Blue Room*, released less than a year later, Gloria Stuart's character tells William Janney's character, "Oh, it must be terrible to be a man and have to be brave. Thank goodness I can be a coward with a clean conscience!"

Two reports by cinema owners in the December 17, 1932 edition of *The Motion Picture Herald* reveal filmgoers' varying attitudes about *The Old Dark House*. Henry Bettendorf at the Opera House in Foley, Minnesota wrote, "Another one of those spooky pictures enjoyed by some and despised by others." Gerald Stettmund at the

Odeon Theatre in Chandler, Oklahoma commented, "Audiences have become immune to the 'Frankenstein' type of picture even though the producers tell us the public is clamoring for them. This one is mildly amusing and seemed to be 'just another picture.'" Stettmund's judgment of *The Old Dark House* as "mildly amusing" indicates he realized the film's humor was intentional. Perhaps he didn't find the film sensationally funny because he was an American. William K. Everson in *Classics of the Horror Film* speculates that only an English person can truly appreciate *The Old Dark House*. In fact, the film made more money in James Whale's native country than it did in the United States, breaking house records at the Capitol Theatre in London.

Although the film did disappointing business in the States, it was reissued in 1939 with just a few cuts. When Universal's rights to *The Old Dark House* lapsed in 1957, the studio didn't bother to renew them. For years, it was thought that the film was lost. Finally in 1968, a shrunken but printable copy was discovered in Universal's vaults. Since then, the film has been shown on television and in revival theatres and issued on commercial home video. Gloria Stuart, the film's last surviving cast member, even provided commentary for the laserdisc and DVD versions.

Having completed *The Old Dark House*, Boris Karloff went to Metro-Goldwyn-Mayer for his second first billed feature. Unlike the Frankenstein Monster and Morgan, Karloff's character, Dr. Fu Manchu, would speak. For the first time, the actor's elegant lisp would be used to frighten filmgoers. But MGM wasn't only interested in utilizing Karloff's voice. The studio's film *The Mask of Fu Manchu* would exploit a widespread paranoia of White Americans—the "yellow peril."

A poster for Hollywood's first pre-Code horror Dracula *(1931). Note the tag line at the top, suggesting both Dracula's menace and sex appeal. Photo courtesy PHOTOFEST.*

A provocative still of Mr. Hyde (Fredric March) terrorizing Ivy Pierson (Miriam Hopkins) from Dr. Jekyll and Mr. Hyde *(1931). Hyde's dangerous libido, which Robert Louis Stevenson barely hinted at in his book, was boldly dramatized in Rouben Mamoulian's film adaptation. Photo courtesy PHOTOFEST.*

Miscegenation and sadism on display in The Mask of Fu Manchu *(1932): the Oriental megalomaniac Fu Manchu's dark skinned minions whip the innocent and helpless Caucasian Terrence Granville (Charles Starrett), to the delight of Fu's wicked daughter Fah Lo See (Myrna Loy). Photo courtesy PHOTOFEST.*

Perverted science in The Island of Lost Souls *(1932): the diabolical Dr. Moreau (Charles Laughton) gloats over his creation Lota the Panther Woman (Kathleen Burke), plotting to mate her with an unwitting human being. Photo courtesy PHOTOFEST.*

Eric Gorman (Lionel Atwill) menaces his vulnerable and unwilling wife Evelyn (Kathleen Burke) in Murders in the Zoo. *More than any other screen fiend in pre-Code horror, Atwill personified lasciviousness. Photo courtesy PHOTOFEST.*

The vengeful Vitus Werdegast (Bela Lugosi) proceeds to skin the crucified Satanist Hjalmar Poelzig (Boris Karloff) alive in The Black Cat *(1934). This film was the last of Hollywood's pre-Code horrors, bringing this series to a stylishly lurid end. Photo courtesy PHOTOFEST.*

THE MASK OF FU MANCHU [1932]

Released November 5, 1932; A Cosmopolitan Production; Produced and Distributed by Metro-Goldwyn-Mayer; *Director:* **Charles Brabin;** *Screenplay:* **Irene Kuhn, Edgar Allan Woolf, and John Willard;** *Based on the novel by Sax Rohmer; Cinematography:* **Tony Gaudio;** *Art Director:* **Cedric Gibbons;** *Editor:* **Ben Lewis;** *Music:* **William Axt;** *Makeup Department:* **Cecil Holland;** *Special Effects:* **Warren Newcombe;** 67 minutes.

Cast: **Boris Karloff (Dr. Fu Manchu), Lewis Stone (Nayland Smith), Karen Morley (Sheila Barton), Charles Starrett (Terrence Granville), Myrna Loy (Fah Lo See), Jean Hersholt (Von Berg), Lawrence Grant (Sir Lionel Barton), David Torrence (McLeod), Willie Fung (Waiter).**

SYNOPSIS: *Britisher Sir Lionel Barton, who is planning an expedition to find the tomb of Genghis Khan, is abducted by the minions of Chinese warlord Dr. Fu Manchu. Fu plans to find the tomb for his own sinister purposes—to use Khan's sword and mask to lead the Asians in a crusade to destroy White civilization. After unsuccessfully employing bribery and torture to compel Barton to reveal the tomb's whereabouts, Fu kills him. Barton's friend and fellow Britisher Nayland Smith leads the expedition, which includes Lionel's distraught daughter Sheila, and they discover the tomb. Fu and his minions capture Smith, his German colleague Von Berg, Sheila, and her boyfriend Terrence Granville. Fu plans to kill Smith and Von Berg in torture devices, sacrifice Sheila to the Asian gods, and make Terrence a love slave for his daughter Fah Lo See. But Smith frees himself from the trap and rescues Von Berg and Terrence. While Terrence saves Sheila from the sacrifice, Smith and Von Berg stop Fu from carrying out his scheme and destroy him. Smith tosses Khan's cursed sword into the sea.*

The debacle of *Freaks* did not discourage Metro-Goldwyn-Mayer from making more horror films. Unlike physically-malformed people, Sax Rohmer's Oriental fiend Fu Manchu was pure fiction. The evil genius had already proven that he was a marketable Hollywood commodity. Between 1929 and 1931, Paramount produced three Fu Manchu films: *The Mysterious Fu Manchu* (1929), *The Return of Dr. Fu Manchu* (1930), and *Daughter of the Dragon* (1931). Warner Oland, who would later play Charlie Chan at Fox, portrayed Rohmer's master criminal in all three films. Oland's Fu Manchu was not inherently wicked. His hatred of the White race was motivated by the murders of his wife and son in the Boxer Rebellion, a real-life anti-imperialist uprising against Western and Japanese intervention in China. MGM planned *their* Fu Manchu to be thoroughly diabolical without any redeeming qualities.

The Mask of Fu Manchu was billed as a Cosmopolitan Production. This unit was established and headed by William Randolph Hearst in the late 1910s. The media tycoon, who was later the role model for Orson Welles' titular antihero *Citizen Kane* (1941), trumpeted his rabid agenda against the Orientals in his newspapers. He warned his readers about a "yellow peril:" a sinister Oriental conspiracy to destroy White civilization. Many White Americans, perhaps the majority, shared Hearst's prejudices. Anti-Oriental hostility was so strong that it led to national laws that prevented any more Chinese or Japanese from immigrating to the United States.

Although Hearst was anxious to alert White American moviegoers about the yellow peril, his company's production of *The Mask of Fu Manchu* was chaotic. Boris Karloff later reminisced, "I shall never forget, about a week before we started, I kept asking for a script—and I was met with roars of laughter at the idea that there would be a script. On the morning that we started shooting, I went into the makeup shop and worked there for about a couple of hours getting this extremely bad makeup on, as a matter of fact, for Fu Manchu. It was ridiculous. And, as I was in the makeup chair, a gentleman came in and handed me about four sheets of paper which was one enormous, long speech. That was to be the opening shot in the film and I was seeing it for the first time, then and there. It was written in the most impeccable English. Then, I said, 'This is absolute nonsense. I can't learn this in time to do it,' and he said, 'Well, it will be all right. Don't worry.' So I got my makeup on and, on my way to the stage from the makeup shop, I was intercepted by somebody else who took those pages away from me and gave me some others that were written in pidgin English!'"

In the finished film, Karloff's Fu Manchu speaks in perfect English. Oozing icy superciliousness, he tells his captive Sir Lionel Barton (Lawrence Grant), "I am a doctor of philosophy from Edinburgh. I'm a doctor of law from Christ College. I am a doctor of medicine from Harvard. My friends, out of courtesy, call me *Doctor.*" If William Randolph Hearst regarded *Fu Manchu*'s yellow peril motif in earnest, Karloff didn't. Recognizing that his role is a cartoonish bogeyman, Boris delivers it with his tongue in his cheek. With such a playful approach, how can anyone take his threats to destroy White civilization seriously?

Karloff also imbues his character with camp mannerisms, suggesting that his Fu is either homosexual or bisexual. Running his long, talon-like fingernails over the body of his young, good-looking captive Terrence Granville (Charles Starrett), his fascination for him is obvious. And when his daughter Fah Lo See says to Fu, "He is not entirely unhandsome, is he, my father?" the wicked patriarch responds, "For a White man, no." Ed Howard points out in his blog on *Fu Manchu* in *Only the Cinema:*

"The homoerotic current certainly extends to the Black servants who are kept by the Chinese: strapping muscular dark men, half-naked in tiny underwear-like shorts. They stand around looking like statues with their sculpted bodies, and it's hard to look at them without thinking that Fah Lo See, and probably Fu Manchu as well, likes having such models of masculine physicality hanging around."

Myrna Loy as Fu Manchu's equally-sinister daughter Fah Lo See emotes in the same lighthearted manner. She had not yet established herself as a sophisticated comedienne in 1932 and was typecast as femmes fatales, some of them "foreign." In fact, MGM considered her for the part of Cleopatra in *Freaks*, but she turned it down, refusing to play a woman being turned into a "freak." The role of Fah Lo See shocked her as much as the role of Cleopatra. Years after she acted in *The Mask of Fu Manchu*, she recalled, "... I had been reading a little Freud ... so I called the director over one day and said, 'Say this is obscene. This woman is a sadistic nymphomaniac!' And he said, 'What does *that* mean?' I mean, we did it all before these kids today ever thought of it, and we didn't even know what we were *doing!*"

To call Fah Lo See a sadistic nymphomaniac is an understatement. Words can't describe her depravity; one has to see her in *The Mask of Fu Manchu*. In one scene, she orders her father's minions to whip Terrence. As she watches the henchmen rip off the young man's shirt, Fah's eyes gleam with pleasure. Her ardor intensifies when she sees the minions lash at the bound Terrence. "Faster!" she repeatedly yells. (In an early draft of the scenario, Fah was even more sadistic, doing the whipping herself.) This scene is supposed to be horrifying. One suspects that some perverted Depression-era filmgoers, both male and female, secretly shared Fah's delight in seeing the topless, tied-up, and tortured Terrence.

Charles Starrett's beefcake physique is further exploited when his unconscious character, wearing only a loincloth, is chained to a table. Fu Manchu concocts a drug to rob Terrence of his free will. The Mandarin fiend gloats to his comatose victim, "I am only going to give you the very smallest amount which will pass off in a short time, because I want you to be your very self when I hand you over to my gentle daughter." Fu Manchu's concoction of the drug remains disturbing viewing today. First, he uses a needle to draw blood from a tarantula, pouring the fluid into a tube. He then uses a poisonous snake to bite one of his minions. Fu extracts the venom from his victim to put in the same tube. What is truly grim viewing is the minion's reaction. He screams, then his mouth remains open in mute agony. Eventually, the man falls down dead in one of pre-Code horror's most disturbing scenes.

When Fu subjects Terrence to his potion, the White man lustfully eyes Fah, obviously playing on White Americans' fears of miscegenation. But Karloff and Starrett had trouble keeping their faces straight when filming the drugging scene. Starrett told Karloff biographer

Cynthia Lindsay, "Boris . . . as Fu Manchu was about to inject a hypodermic needle into the back of my neck—we couldn't get it right—it never looked like the real thing—so the director . . . suddenly yelled, 'I've got it!' He sent to the commissary four especially-baked potatoes—he tucked one of them into the collar of my shirt and said to Boris, 'Go ahead—jab it in—it can't hurt him—it will only go into the potato.' We started the scene. Boris plunged the needle into (allegedly) my neck—the potato exploded with a great pop, got all over Boris and all over me. The two of us couldn't stop laughing—we went through three more takes, using up the rest of the potatoes with the same results until we were hysterical. Finally, the director said, 'You two just go home—you're no use—we'll shoot it in the morning!'"

The Mask of Fu Manchu required far more shooting than MGM planned. The studio brass, after viewing the first rushes, considered them too horrific for public consumption. Considering how gruesome the released version is, one can only imagine what the original cut was like. Anxious to avoid a *Freaks*-like disaster, MGM's front office shut down the production. *The New York Times* reported, "The Chinese picture has been halted, while the story is being rewritten, several of the writers having been formed into a shock-troop to get something filmable out in a hurry."

The "the original director of the "Chinese picture," Charles Vidor, was fired and replaced by Charles Brabin. Ironically, Brabin had been dismissed from his directing assignment of MGM's *Rasputin and the Empress* and was replaced by Richard Boleslawski. This historical drama was the only film to feature all of the Barrymore siblings, John, Lionel, and Ethel. Ethel constantly argued with Brabin on how to play the role of Czarina Alexandra. She kept reminding him, "I knew her majesty personally." Fed up with him, Ethel phoned Louis B. Mayer on the soundstage, declaring, "See here, Mayer, let's get rid of this Brahbin or Braybin or what's-his-name." With Brabin replacing Vidor on *The Mask of Fu Manchu*, the production was somehow completed.

Terrence was supposed to strangle Fah Lo See when she tried to stab him. But since Myrna Loy was a rising star, MGM decided that filmgoers would be unhappy to see her character strangled. Fah

Lo See's death scene was eliminated from the final cut. Her fate, like Hercules' in *Freaks*, is a mystery.

Fu Manchu's publicity department pandered to White filmgoers' paranoia over the yellow peril. A promo copy announced, "Mad Oriental tortures! Crazed, heartless desires! This Oriental monster almost wrecked civilization with his love-drug." The publicity department also catered to the filmgoers' morbid curiosities. Another promo copy featured illustrations of Fu's various tortures: "The Bell That Never Stops! The Wall of Knives! Closer—to the Jaws of the Crocodiles! The Serum That Enslaves!" Nayland Smith (Lewis Stone) was originally supposed to be threatened to be impaled by the knives. But the portly Von Berg (Jean Hersholt) was subjected to this death trap in the released cut; the filmmakers assumed a fat man was more vulnerable to the knives than a thin one. Nayland Smith was instead menaced by the crocodiles.

Some reviewers believed that *Fu Manchu*'s shocks were too excessive to be effective. The Los Angeles *Record* commented, "The picture is so packed with underground passages, electrical death machines, snakes, tarantulas . . . hypnotizing serums, daggers in the back, trap doors, screams, smoking fluids, mummies coming to life, and all the other gasp accessories that the audience was unable to do anything but laugh." *Variety* noted, "The diabolical stuff is piled on so thick at the finish, audiences are liable to laugh where they oughtn't. The audience at the Capitol [in New York, NY] did."

Critics' commentary on *Fu Manchu*'s suitability for youngsters varied. *The Educational Screen* denounced the film as "stupid" and did not recommend it for children and teenagers. "Absurd piling up of artificial horrors—animal, mechanical, electrical, chemical—till drama and character interest are buried," the writer sneered. "Naive nightmare by and for elementary minds." *Modern Screen* opined, ". . . if you don't mind the children seeing such exciting stuff, it's okay for them." Whatever reservations the reviewers had about *Fu Manchu*, their opinions did not hurt the film's box office performance. It made a profit, probably because of the popularity of Sax Rohmer's character. The film's success also further solidified Boris Karloff's status as a horror star.

The Chinese government was incensed by *The Mask of Fu Manchu*, considering it an insult to the Chinese people. Determined to persuade Hollywood to stop presenting negative Chinese portrayals, the government set up a vice consulate in Los Angeles. *Variety* reported that its "chief duty will be to contact the studios and suggest to them the getting of proper atmosphere, and present the Chinese in a proper light in forthcoming pictures." The motion picture industry was not immediately receptive.

Even after the Production Code was strengthened, Hollywood continued to capitalize on White Americans' fear of the yellow peril. In 1935, the low-budget studio Monogram released a Fu Manchu knockoff called *The Mysterious Mr. Wong*, with Bela Lugosi in the title role of the Chinese fiend. This film is littered with casual anti-Oriental quotes. The most notorious one occurs when a White character learns of a Chinese person's death: "Better dead ones than live ones." Eventually, Hollywood's portrayals of the Chinese became more positive, mainly because China became an American ally against the Japanese during World War II. (In contrast, the Japanese were demonized in films during the war, and only after the conflict ended did Hollywood depict them more fairly.)

One can still enjoy *The Mask of Fu Manchu* today, particularly because of Karloff and Loy's entertaining villainy. But only if he or she doesn't take anything seriously; the movie is an appalling work of anti-Oriental propaganda. All the Orientals in *Fu Manchu* are either fiends, degenerates, or fools. Fu Manchu's climactic speech to his followers just before they are defeated by Nayland Smith and his friends sums up White Americans' paranoia: "Kill the White man and take his women!" Fu and his followers are also evil because they are not Christians. The Mandarin fiend mocks his White captives' piety, sneering that they "will have the pleasure of entering your Christian heaven together."

Nayland Smith and the other Whites do not mince words in expressing their fear and mistrust of Orientals. When Smith warns his friends that Fu has spies, he adds, "I can't even trust our own coolies." He also worries about Lionel's daughter Sheila (Karen Morley): "Do you suppose for a moment Fu Manchu doesn't know we have a beautiful White girl here with us?" Sheila herself hurls a racial slur at Fu, calling him "you hideous yellow monster!" Smith's most revealing statement is "Will we ever understand these Eastern races? Will we ever learn anything?" This quote inadvertently helps explain why White Americans feared the Orientals; they *didn't* understand them.

The Mask of Fu Manchu also illustrates Hollywood's discrimination against Oriental actors. All of the major Oriental roles, particularly Fu Manchu and Fah Lo See, are played by Caucasians in yellowface. Boris Karloff would be cast as an Oriental in subsequent films, although never as such a horrendous caricature as Fu Manchu. Ironically, during the unofficial ban on horror films in the late 1930s, he starred as the heroic Chinese detective Mr. Wong (not to be confused with Bela Lugosi's *nefarious* Mr. Wong) in a mystery series released by Monogram. Perhaps the English actor considered the Mr. Wong series a sort of atonement for his participation in *The Mask of Fu Manchu.* When horror came back in vogue, however, Monogram cast genuine Oriental actor Keye Luke in the final Mr. Wong film while starring Karloff in the mad scientist film *The Ape.*

Back in 1932, Karloff had returned to Universal after completing *The Mask of Fu Manchu.* Carl Laemmle, Sr.'s studio planned to exploit the actor's voice in a new horror film, *The Mummy.* Karloff's role, the resurrected Imhotep, would be more challenging and rewarding than Fu Manchu. Imhotep was not a comic book arch-villain but a complicated character, both a ruthless killer and a gallant lover. *The Mummy's* shocks would be, for the most part, tastefully and stylishly handled. If *The Mask of Fu Manchu* was the cinematic equivalent of a tabloid screed, *The Mummy* would be the equivalent of an elegant poem.

THE MUMMY (1932)

Released December 22, 1932; A Universal Picture; *Director:* **Karl Freund;** *Producer:* **Carl Laemmle, Jr.;** *Associate Producer:* **Stanley Bergerman;** *Screenplay:* **John L. Balderston;** *Story:* **Nina Wilcox Putnam and Richard Schayer;** *Photography:* **Charles Stumar;** *Editor:* **Milton Carruth;** *Art Director:* **Willy Pogany;** *Music:* **James Dietrich;** *Special Effects:* **John P. Fulton;** *Makeup:* **Jack P. Pierce; 72 minutes.**

Cast: **Boris Karloff (Imhotep/Ardath Bey), Zita Johann (Helen Grosvenor/Princess Anck-es-en-Amon), David Manners (Frank Whemple), Edward Van Sloan (Dr. Muller), Arthur Byron (Sir Joseph Whemple), Bramwell Fletcher (Ralph Norton), Noble Johnson (The Nubian), Kathryn Byron (Frau Muller), Leonard Mudie (Prof. Pearson), James Crane (King Amenophis), Eddie Kane (Dr. LeBarron).**

SYNOPSIS: In 1921, Sir Joseph Whemple leads a British expedition in Egypt which discovers the mummified corpse of the high priest Imhotep in a tomb. Also discovered there is an ancient document called the Scroll of Thoth, which according to ancient Egyptian folklore was used to revive the dead. When Whemple's assistant Ralph Norton reads the document, he inadvertently resurrects Imhotep. Seeing Imhotep go off with the Scroll, Ralph goes mad. Eleven years later, Joseph's son Frank is on another expedition. A wizened looking Egyptian who calls himself Ardath Bey (actually Imhotep) informs Frank about the unplundered tomb of the ancient Egyptian Princess Anck-es-en-Amon. When the tomb is unearthed, Anck-es-en-Amon's coffin is placed in the Cairo museum. There, Bey uses the Scroll of Thoth to try to revive his love, the Princess. He telepathically summons a young woman named Helen Grosvenor, who is the reincarnation of Anck-es-en-Amon.

Frank falls in love with Helen, but Bey tries to kill him. He plans to transfer Helen's soul to Anck-es-en-Amon's body. But Helen refuses to sacrifice her present life to become a mummy like Bey and prays to the Egyptian goddess Isis for help. The goddess Isis intervenes and destroys Bey. Helen and Frank are reunited.

Countless horror fans and scholars have noted that *The Mummy*'s scenario is a thinly-disguised rehash of *Dracula*. In both films, an undead creature uses his supernatural powers to bewitch an innocent woman. The woman's anxious boyfriend and an elderly expert in the occult team up to stop the monster before he can destroy her humanity. The similarity of the two Universal horrors is unsurprising, since John L. Balderston worked on both stories. *Dracula* veterans David Manners and Edward Van Sloan more or less reprise their roles as Jonathan Harker and Professor Van Helsing in *The Mummy*.

Boris Karloff's Imhotep has none of the allure of Bela Lugosi's Dracula. Jack Pierce's meticulously-crafted makeup makes Karloff look every bit the decrepit, embalmed grotesque he's supposed to be. Even without makeup, Karloff wasn't conventionally handsome. He didn't look the romantic type with his heavy brow and his potato shaped nose. In his pre-*Frankenstein* career, Boris tended to be cast as a thug or a rogue. The human Karloff seemed an unlikely lover; the mummified Karloff seems a *repugnant* lover.

Nevertheless, Imhotep's love for Princess Anck-es-en-Amon (Zita Johann) is sincere. Karloff invests his characterization with the same haunting vulnerability and sensitivity he gave to the Frankenstein Monster. Even though he unhesitatingly murders people, Imhotep is not a repellent sex maniac like Lionel Atwill's Eric Gorman in *Murders in the Zoo*. The idea of the withered creature turning the Princess's living reincarnation, Helen Grosvenor (the same actress), into a mummy so he can consummate their relationship is horrifying. But one can't help sympathizing with Imhotep, who has endured centuries of suffering because of his devotion to her.

On the whole, *The Mummy* is a tasteful and restrained pre-Code horror. Most of the killings take place off-screen. The audience witnesses Sir Joseph Whemple (Arthur Byron) suffering a fatal heart attack induced by the mummy. But this death scene is completely bloodless and no more unnerving than countless death scenes in post-Code films.

The Mummy has one gruesome scene during the flashback to ancient Egypt. We see the soldiers hurling spears at the slaves who have buried Imhotep. A brief shot depicts a bleeding and collapsing slave with a spear penetrated through his body. The violence is shown to illustrate Imhotep's off-screen narration: "The slaves were killed so that none should know. The soldiers who killed them were also slain, so no friend could creep to the desert with funeral offerings for my condemned spirit." The slave is a Black man. Since the film is black and white, the blood doesn't greatly contrast with his skin. *The Mummy*'s filmmakers would have gotten into trouble with the Production Code if they depicted a bloodied White slave—the gore on his body would have been far more visible.

Some contemporary critics commented on *The Mummy*'s discreet handling of terror. *The Washington Post* opined, "*The Mummy* . . . is not in any sense a horror picture. Only in the startling realism of his makeup does Boris Karloff recall such [*sic*] of his terrifying earlier pictures, say as *Frankenstein*." The *Hollywood Herald* approvingly declared, "It has most of the thrills of the 'shock' pictures . . . without the gruesomeness of that cycle." *Modern Screen* wrote, ". . . parts of it okay for the children," although it didn't explain which parts weren't okay and why. The columnist for *Variety*'s "Woman's Angle" was unoffended if condescending: "Pallid Dracula, safe for the kids. Too mild to upset the ladies as its predecessors have done."

Despite *The Mummy*'s unwholesome concept of an ancient, crumbling man in love with a young, healthy woman, the sexual angle is handled delicately. In the climax, Imhotep grabs Helen, now possessed by the soul of Anck-es-en-Amon, in order to transfer her spirit to the princess's mummified body. "It is not lawful for me, a priestess of Isis, to see or touch an unclean thing," she declares, and she pulls away from him. Director Karl Freund gives the audience a close-up of Helen's arm, stained with Imhotep's rotting flesh. She realizes that Imhotep is a living cadaver and he plans to make her one, too. "I loved you once but now you belong with the dead!" she cries. "I am Anck-es-en-Amon but I . . . I'm somebody else, too! I want to live, even in this strange new world." So she prays to Isis for help and the goddess destroys Imhotep.

For most of the time she appears in *The Mummy*, Zita Johann is not provocatively attired. In her first scene in bed, upset by Imhotep's hold over her, one of the shoulder straps of her nightgown is halfway down on her arm, indicating her distraught state. After a scene of Muller, Frank, and Dr. LeBarron (Eddie Kane) discussing her condition, Freund returns to Johann's bedridden scene. She is now composed, and both shoulder straps are neatly in place.

In the climax, Johann looks alluring in ancient Egyptian finery. Attired in a filmy gown with only a metal breastplate covering her upper region and sporting a headdress over a curly black wig, she looks, in Gregory William Mank's words, "like she just sashayed off the stage of a Cairo strip parlor." Her navel is concealed, but when she struggles with Imhotep's Nubian slave (Noble Johnson) and her headdress slips off, part of her midriff is exposed. When the Production Code was revised in 1934, the navel could no longer be displayed on the screen. It wasn't until the 1960s when the Code collapsed that belly buttons could be showcased!

The Motion Picture Herald published a suggestive two-page ad for *The Mummy* a week before its release. A picture of Johann in an evening gown stood alongside the text, "The living eyes blazed like balls of fire and fastened their hungry gaze on the gorgeous creature!" In the film, when Imhotep uses his hypnotic powers, his orbs do look like they're emanating light. (This same technique was used for Bela Lugosi twice, ineptly in *Dracula* and adroitly in *White Zombie*.) But *The Motion Picture Herald*'s implication that the Mummy lusts for Zita Johann's character is misleading. His feelings for her are tender and courtly. When he first sees her as Helen Grosvenor, Karloff gazes at her with a sad longing.

Tom Johnson speculates in *Censored Screams* that *The Mummy*'s theme of reincarnation may not have played well in Middle America. But if so, it didn't torpedo the film's box office performance; it eventually made a profit of $140,000. When the Production Code was given teeth, the subject of reincarnation was not banished from the screen. This theme was absent from Universal's first two post-Code Mummy films, *The Mummy's Hand* (1940) and *The Mummy's*

Tomb (1942), but it was revived in the following movies *The Mummy's Ghost* and *The Mummy's Curse*, both released in 1944.

Zita Johann, who played the Egyptian Princess and her modern alter ego, fervently believed in reincarnation. In her later years, she lived in an old house in West Nyack, New York, which was built before the American Revolution. Zita claimed that in a previous life she had died there. Karl Freund made her experience on the set a grueling hell, and she believed this resulted in her near death experience during filming.

Freund was on edge because *The Mummy* was his first directorial assignment. Johann recalled, "He felt he needed a scapegoat in case he didn't come in on schedule ... Well, *I* was cast as the scapegoat—and I saw through it right away!" Freund harassed her by claiming she had to do a scene naked from the waist up. Zita's secretary Ruby and chauffeur Sasha tried to protect her from the director's abuses, but they eventually took their toll. While playing a scene with Karloff one late Saturday night, she passed out. As Zita slipped out of consciousness, she heard one member of the crew say, "What that son-of-a-bitch has done to her!" She remained out cold for an hour. Zita later recalled, "They couldn't get a doctor—it was eleven o'clock at night. So the crew prayed me back to consciousness." Boris, still in his makeup, expressed concern: "Zita, darling—are you all right?"

The actor never publicly spoke about the incident, but it must have left a strong impression. The following year, when film actors established their own union, the Screen Actors Guild, Karloff joined it and became one of its staunchest advocates. He continued to work at Universal, but he irked the studio management by insisting on only working eight hours a day. And his opinion of his bosses remained low. In 1935, during filming of *The Raven*, supporting actor Ian Wolfe asked Karloff where the toilet was. "This *whole* place," Boris replied, referring to Universal, "is a toilet!"

If there were big problems during *The Mummy*'s filming, the film's release generated no major controversies or protests. The same could not be said for Paramount's coming shocker, *The Island of Lost Souls*. Like *Dr. Jekyll and Mr. Hyde*, this film was adapted from an esteemed literary work. But *Island of Lost Souls* would not enjoy great prestige or popularity, managing to offend both censors and moviegoers. And even H.G. Wells, the author of the book on which it was based, *The Island of Dr. Moreau*, would denounce *The Island of Lost Souls*.

THE ISLAND OF LOST SOULS [1932]

Released December 23, 1932 by Paramount; *Director:* **Erle C. Kenton;** *Screenplay:* **Waldemar Young and Philip Wylie,** *based on H.G. Wells's novel* **The Island of Dr. Moreau;** *Photography:* **Karl Struss;** *Art Director:* **Hans Dreier;** *Special Photographic Effects:* **Gordon Jennings;** *Makeup:* **Wally Westmore; 72 minutes.**

Cast: **Charles Laughton (Dr. Moreau), Richard Arlen (Edward Parker), Leila Hyams (Ruth Thomas), Bela Lugosi (Sayer of the Law), Kathleen Burke (Lota, the Panther Woman), Arthur Hohl (Montgomery), Stanley Fields (Captain Davies), Paul Hurst (Captain Donahue), Hans Steinke (Ouran), Tetsu Komai (M'Ling), George Irving (The American Consul).**

SYNOPSIS: Edward Parker, a survivor of a shipwreck, is rescued and nursed back to health by a physician named Montgomery on the trading ship S.S. Covena. This ship is taking animals to a South Sea Island ruled by renegade scientist Dr. Moreau. Montgomery, who is on the lam for an unspecified crime, works for Moreau. The recovered Parker gets into a fight with the drunken Captain Davies when he protests the sea captain's mistreatment of an assistant of Montgomery's. When Davies drops off Montgomery, his assistant, and the animals on Moreau's island, he also spitefully drops off Parker. At first, Moreau objects but then decides that Parker would be an ideal mate for his creation, Lota the Panther Woman. Lota, along with other creatures including the abused assistant, are "manimals," evolved from beasts through Moreau and Montgomery's experiments. Moreau controls his creatures by masquerading as an immortal god and making them recite a law that forbids them from walk-

ing on fours and spilling blood. If any of the creatures show signs of regressing to their zoological origins, the doctor places them in a laboratory called the House of Pain to burn the animal out of them. Meanwhile, Parker's concerned fiancée Ruth Thomas asks the American Consul about Parker's whereabouts. He sends her with a Captain Donahue in another ship to Moreau's island. Since Parker has learned of Lota's feline origins and is no longer attracted to her, Moreau tries to get another manimal, Ouran, to ravage Ruth. Before the creature can violate her, Parker scares him off with a gun. When Montgomery learns about the doctor's scheme, he is so appalled that he refuses to work with Moreau any more. When Donahue tries to gather the other visitors to leave the island, Moreau orders Ouran to kill him. Ouran and the other manimals realize the human Moreau is mortal like the human Donahue, and they vivisect him in the House of Pain. Lota is killed by another manimal, but Parker, Ruth, and Montgomery escape from the island.

When H.G. Wells' novel *The Island of Dr. Moreau* was published in 1896, some literary critics (though not all) found it repellent. One reviewer in the *Athenaeum* declared, "The horrors described by Mr. Wells ... very pertinently raise the question how far it is legitimate to create feelings of disgust in a work of art." Wells intended his book to be an allegory of the fragility of human civilization, and he resented the reviewers' condemnations. In an 1897 interview for the journal *The Young Man*, the author contended, "I should say that *The Island of Dr. Moreau*, although it was written in a great hurry and is marred by many faults, is the best work I have done. It has been stupidly dealt with—as a mere shocker—by people who ought to have known better."

Ironically, Wells joined the outcry of protestors of Paramount's film adaptation *The Island of Lost Souls*. He accused the studio of overemphasizing the horror at the expense of its philosophical content. The author was enraged that scenarists Waldemar Young and Philip Wylie spiced up the plot with a proposed mating between the castaway Edward Parker (Richard Arlen) and Moreau's creation Lota the Panther Woman (Kathleen Burke). Paramount *did* dilute Wells' sociological message. Although the film addresses the hazards of careless and unethical experimentation, it does not use the doctor's island of manimals as a microcosm of the fragile human society.

The screenwriters' bestiality angle, however, is not gratuitous kinkiness. Dr. Moreau (Charles Laughton) hopes that if Lota and Parker successfully procreate, this will prove that the Panther Woman is a fully-developed human without any zoological traits. The scientist is upset when "the stubborn beast flesh" (Moreau's description) reemerges. He vows to continue to experiment on Lota so he can "burn the animal out of her." The doctor himself has no carnal interest in her; indeed, he has no regard for her feelings. To him, Lota is only a test subject to prove his theory on evolving animals into people.

When Parker's fiancée Ruth Thomas (Leila Hyams) arrives on the island, the wicked doctor goads a male creation, Ouran (Hans Steinke), into trying to rape her. This is a crucial plot point that portends Moreau's downfall. Grimly determined to validate his hypothesis, he becomes even more brutal and reckless. When his accomplice Montgomery (Arthur Hohl) learns of Moreau's plan for Ruth, he declares, "I know you too well and too long, Moreau. I've stood for anything. I have stood for plenty. But not this. You're insane to even think of it, and I'm through with you here and now."

The cinematic Montgomery, unlike his literary counterpart, does not perish. Since this character sincerely repents his sins and decides to service his jail sentence in England, the screenplay spares him. Moreau, on the other hand, is killed by his own creations because he never acknowledges the evils in his experimentations. Incidentally, the film never explains Montgomery's crime which caused him to flee to Moreau's faraway island. The scientist tells Parker that his assistant was charged with a "professional indiscretion." Depression-era filmgoers might imagine a variety of lurid interpretations for this cryptic term.

The scantily-clad and curvaceous Kathleen Burke is a provocative sight as Lota the Panther Woman. (She later recalled it was an ordeal for her to work on the cold jungle set "dressed in a sting of beads and a strip of silk.") In *Women in Horror Films, 1930s,*

Gregory William Mank describes her outlandish appearance: "The wildly-teased hair, the giant raccoon eyes ringed in mascara, the lipsticked, bee-stung lips . . . Kathleen Burke's Lota looks like a 1932 hooker, all dressed up for a 'John' with a South Seas fetish." One can easily understand Parker's attraction to her and the other manimals' lust for her.

A former Chicago dental assistant, Burke was the winner of Paramount's "Panther Woman" contest, beating thousands of competitors. (Indeed, she was billed as "The Panther Woman" in the film's opening credits.) She passed all of the contest's stipulations. One of these was a written endorsement by two citizens asserting her good moral standing in the community. As Mank points out in *The Very Witching Time of Night*, that requirement seemed hypocritical "considering the nature of the sexed-up films that Paramount was producing at this time!"

Paramount's publicity department exploited Burke's sex appeal. Illustrations of the actress' provocative figure appeared in *Island*'s advertisements. A few drawings depicted her topless, her breasts barely concealed by a necklace and her long hair. The text in these advertisements was both suggestive and kinky. One can imagine the reformers' outrage if they read this teaser: "She Was His Masterpiece! Woman Out of Panther . . . Lota was all Woman. Her Flesh Soft and Warm; Her Eyes Tender With Love; Her Lips Inviting. Yet Forever Cursed With the Strain of the Jungle, Forever Barred from a Woman's Fulfillment!"

Leila Hyams, *Island*'s other major female player (and a veteran cast member of *Freaks*.) is properly attired for most of her screen time. But before Ouran tries to invade her boudoir (Parker scares him away with his gun), he watches her strip to her underwear and pull down her stockings. As with Madge Bellamy's scene in her lingerie in *White Zombie*, Leila's underdressed appearance emphasizes her character's vulnerability to dark, unearthly forces. Significantly, she doesn't know that Ouran is spying on her. Director Erle C. Kenton adeptly uses this peeping Tom segment to build up to the attempted rape scene.

Most of *Island*'s violence is suggestive rather than explicit, but the film does have some grisly images. Parker witnesses Moreau and

Montgomery vivisecting one of the manimals in the laboratory, the House of Pain. The sight is brief, but the victim's tortured screams linger in the mind. This scene recalls Dr. Mirakle's experiment on the prostitute in *Murders in the Rue Morgue*; that scene was also shocking because of the victim's cries.

When the manimals rebel against Moreau, the doctor whips them. The audience sees a few creatures bear the brunt of his lash. But the manimals don't flinch, and continue to menace him. The Sayer of the Law (Bela Lugosi) has declared, "Law no more!" so the whip no longer intimidates them.

When Lota battles one of the beast men, resulting in both their deaths, she is seen strangling the creature. Had *Island of Lost Souls* been made after the Code was strengthened, the censors would have not allowed the filmmakers such a blatant image. Nor would they have allowed them the dead manimal's bloodied face to be shown. The filmmakers do not depict the manimals' dissection of Moreau. No depiction is necessary; the doctor's agonized screams are enough.

Like H.G. Wells' book and like the film *Murders in the Rue Morgue*, *Island of Lost Souls* explores Charles Darwin's evolution theory. Dr. Moreau explains to Parker his motivation for creating the manimals: "Man is the present climax of a long process of organic revolution. All animal life is tending toward the human form." Citing his experiments to metamorphize beasts into people, the doctor boasts that he has "wiped out hundreds of thousands of years of evolution." Religious groups who disputed Darwin's theory might have recoiled from the film's premise. When Paramount contacted the strengthened Production Code to rerelease the movie in 1935, Moreau's dialogue about scientific human development was deleted.

Even during the production of *Island*, the Production Code expressed qualms. Jason Joy told Paramount, "I assume that some thought has been given to the possibility of injecting the idea of crossing animals with humans. If this is the case it is my opinion that all such thought should be abandoned, for I am sure you would never be permitted to suggest that sort of thing on the screen." Not only did the studio ignore Joy's warning, but the cross-breeding theme was used in post-Code horror films. For instance, in *The Mad Monster* (1942), demented doctor George Zucco injects a mixture of wolf and human blood into his unwitting guinea pig (Glenn Strange), making him a werewolf. In *Captive Wild Woman* (1943), mad scientist John Carradine transplants human glands into a gorilla and gives her a human brain, turning her into a voluptuous woman (Acquanetta). Like Lota, Carradine's creation pines for a handsome man (Millburn Stone).

When the film was released, most of the state censorship boards approved its showing. The exception was Virginia; the board's director R.C.L. Moncure judged the film too extreme for public viewing. Paramount officials considered fighting the ban in court. They didn't have to; Moncure eventually permitted the film to be screened in his state. But Virginia's censors made some considerable cuts to the movie before allowing moviegoers to see it.

At first, *Island* attracted many moviegoers. The film did particularly good business when it opened in the Rialto in New York City on January 12, 1933. Kate Cameron wrote in the *New York Daily News* that it was the "longest queue I've seen along the rialto [sic] in over a year." So many New Yorkers came to the Rialto because they could now afford to; ticket prices had just been slashed. Paramount issued a poster boasting the film's successful New York City opening with the heading "Something NEW hits blasé B'way!"

In ballyhooing *Island's* Manhattan premiere, the Rialto avoided the film's horror angle to concentrate on the sultry Panther Woman. According to an article in *Variety*, Sam Dembow, who managed a chain of Paramount's theaters, "decided that the chiller thing had been done to death in every way. Paramount had spent much time and expense exploiting the Panther Woman angle, including a contest, and it was also believed that this should be cashed on." This marketing strategy seemed to work at first. A subsequent *Variety* article noted about *Island*, "In theatres where it's been sold from the Panther Girl side, draw has been better than where sold as another chiller."

However, *Variety*'s column "The Woman's Angle" was disapproving, forecasting the film's box office decline: "Chills of distaste at the hideousness of this shocker's men-made-out-of-animals are not the kind of chills ladies like in pictures." Some critics were openly ill at ease. *The Film Daily*'s reviewer wrote, "The spectacle of Charles Laughton, as a queer scientist, practicing surgery on animals in order to create a new type of human being, and succeeding only in turning out a fearful flock of monstrosities, probably has its appeal for horror fans, but as family entertainment it is not a pleasant order." Philip K. Scheuer of the *Los Angeles Times* considered *Island* to be "horrible to the point of repugnance."

Many people, having read *Island*'s press materials, must have shared Scheuer's apprehensions. As the film continued to play in theaters, attendance figures dropped. A March 21 *Variety* column reported that last week's box office performance in Lincoln, Nebraska was lackluster because it was "too freaky to draw." A lot of White Americans may have found Burke's Panther Woman to be too alien to appeal to them. In her "Going Places" column in the same publication, Cecilia Ager unfavorably contrasted her to Lelia Hyams' heroine: "Lelia Hyams' wholesomeness has never been so welcome as in this murky island. A clear light of sanity, she illuminates the dank proceedings with her good common sense and clean cut Nordic face." The attraction between the savage Panther Woman and the Anglo-Saxon Edward Parker must have seemed like miscegenation to Depression-era filmgoers, which they considered to be as immoral as bestiality.

Despite Paramount's tireless publicity efforts, *Island of Lost Souls* was a box office disappointment. The film's financial prospects were further hindered when several "foreign" countries banned it from public showings. The United Kingdom was one of them, damning it as "too horrible." As *Variety* noted, this was "a blow to Paramount, because the picture was made from an H.G. Wells story and features Charles Laughton, both British." Wells, who despised the film's adaptation, must have privately chortled when his native country rejected it.

Hollywood still believed that the American public demanded more horror films. A minor studio named Majestic prepared another mad scientist film. It would be far less controversial than *Island*; it was not adapted from a living author's famous story, and its horrors were comparatively mild. This film, *The Vampire Bat*, would not create a lasting impression for filmgoers. But it was a turning point for Lionel Atwill. For the first time, he would play the villain in a horror film. Like Bela Lugosi and Boris Karloff, Atwill would be typecast on the screen as a bogeyman, the "Maddest Doctor of Them All," as horror aficionado Forrest J. Ackerman called him.

THE VAMPIRE BAT [1933]

Released on January 17, 1933 by Majestic; *Director:* **Frank Strayer;** *Producer:* **Phil Goldstone;** *Screenplay:* **Edward T. Lowe;** *Photographer:* **Ira Morgan;** *Art Director:* **Daniel Hall;** *Editor:* **Otis Garrett; 62 minutes.**

Cast: **Lionel Atwill (Otto von Niemann), Fay Wray (Ruth Berlin), Melvyn Douglas (Karl Bretschneider), Maude Eburne (Gussie Schnappman), George E. Stone (Kringen), Dwight Frye (Herman Gleib), Robert Frazer (Emil Borst), Rita Carlisle (Martha Mueller), Lionel Belmore (Gustav Schoen), William V. Mong (Sauer), Stella Adams (Georgianna), Harrison Greene (Weingarten).**

SYNOPSIS: A series of mysterious murders has occurred in the Middle European village of Kleinschloss. The villagers fear a vampire is on the loose. They suspect Herman Gleib, an unkempt simpleton who is fascinated by bats. Scientist Dr. Otto von Niemann professes the likelihood of a vampire, but Inspector Karl Bretschneider scoffs at the concept. After two more killings, the villagers pursue Herman, causing him to jump to his death. Niemann is actually responsible for the killings; he hypnotizes his assistant Emil Borst to commit these crimes and then drains the victims' blood to make living tissue. When Otto's secretary Ruth Berlin learns of this, he bounds and gags her. But Karl, Ruth's fiancée, learns about Otto's scheme and rescues her. Emil recovers from Otto's spell and, learning about the crimes, kills the scientist and himself.

Unlike other pre-Code horrors released around the same time, *The Vampire Bat* hasn't greatly impressed film fans and scholars. The general consensus is that the Poverty Row (the name given to minor, low-budget studios like Majestic) chiller is competently made but unremarkable, despite its good cast. Indeed, *The Vampire Bat* is the least memorable of all the pre-Code horrors.

Professor Niemann's creation, a sponge that only breathes, is a far cry from Dr. Frankenstein's monster and Dr. Moreau's manimals. The mad doctor's undoing is presented in a rushed and perfunctory way. The filmmakers don't bother to show him and his accomplice Emil killing each other; they just show Karl and Ruth hearing gunshots. It is unlikely that director Frank Strayer and his crew worried they would offend audiences with graphic violence; their tepid handling of Niemann and Emil's deaths was probably due to a combination of a low budget and a lack of creativity.

The Vampire Bat does have one graphic shocker. The audience sees blood drained from one of Niemann's victims flowing into a glass container. Had the film been made in Technicolor, the censors may not have permitted such a ghastly image. As for the victim, Niemann's housekeeper Georgianna (Stella Adams), she is trussed up like a crucifixion image, her arms outstretched. The filmmakers were probably inspired by Arlene Francis's "crucifixion" by Dr. Mirakle in *Murders in the Rue Morgue*.

Otherwise, the film's luridness is suggested, rather than shown. But Gustav Schoen, the Burgermeister (Lionel Belmore), describes in grisly detail the corpses' puncture marks: "Two wounds on the neck, right at the jugular vein . . . pierced and spread apart just as if two fang-like teeth had been through the flesh and right into the vein. And in every case, a blood clot—eight inches from the victim's neck." Belmore's vivid elucidation, passionately delivered, conjures palpable grotesqueries in the imagination. Had the Code been enforced at the time of *Vampire Bat*'s making, the censors would have probably demanded that the filmmakers tone it down.

In a generally-favorable review in *Motion Picture Herald*, the writer, credited only with the surname "Aaronson," commented, "Gruesomeness has been reduced to a minimum, the narrative relying more on implication than facts to indicate the horrible." But Aaronson did not recommend *The Vampire Bat* for all ages: "It would perhaps be much better if the youngsters did not see the picture." Perhaps this critic worried that even implied shocks could traumatize young viewers.

Variety's "Woman's Angle" column, tailored to female filmgoers, contended, "Despite its gruesome photography and good cast, fails to terrorize the ladies. [Sic] Because of its soporific, carelessly-developed story, pieced together from type predecessors." This review indicated that female movie patrons, then as now, enjoyed being scared. By the end of 1936, horror films were temporarily banned, so women had to get their pleasurable chills from reading and listening to the radio.

Since the audience isn't supposed to learn Atwill's character is the culprit until late in *The Vampire Bat*, the actor eschews sinister or kinky shadings during much of the film's running time. This starkly contrasts with Atwill's performance in *Doctor X*, where as a red herring, he played up the twisted nuances until the climax. Once his character's guilt is exposed in *Vampire Bat*, Lionel milks his character's nefariousness to the hilt.

Unlike his later portrayal of Eric Gorman in *Murders in the Zoo*, Otto Niemann is not a sex fiend. He is a standard mad scientist who rationalizes his dastardly work: " ... what are a few lives to be weighed in the balance against the achievements of biological science?" Still, Atwill infuses his part with a lascivious streak. Toward the end of his tirade at Ruth (Fay Wray), he approaches her menacingly, his eyes burning with lust.

Even if *The Vampire Bat* had been made in the post-Code era, Atwill would have been able to spice up his mad doctor role with lecherous overtones. In the 1941 Universal chiller *Man Made Monster*, Atwill is a scientist who turns Lon Chaney, Jr. into a mindless creature who fatally electrocutes anyone he touches. In the film's climax, he plans to make Anne Nagel a freak like Chaney. Leering at the lovely woman, Atwill declares, "You know, it's a curious fact that ever since my earliest experiments with rabbits and guinea pigs, I've always found the female of the species was more sensitive to electrical impulse than the male!" Charles Laughton once said, "They can't censor the gleam in my eye." Similarly, the Production Code couldn't censor Atwill.

The Vampire Bat's setting is a fanciful European village, far removed from the grim realities of Depression-era America. But the movie touches on the issues of prejudice and vigilantism. The townspeople suspect the mentally challenged Herman Glieb (Dwight Frye) is the murderer. No one has seen him kill anyone, but he's a deviant in their eyes because of his unkempt appearance and his affection for bats. Karl (Melvyn Douglas) warns the other villagers not to jump to conclusions: "Herman wouldn't hurt a baby and you know it!" Even when circumstantial evidence points to the feeble-minded misfit and Karl reluctantly decides Herman should be taken into custody, he orders the villagers not to hurt him.

However, when the overzealous mob corners Herman in a cave, they frighten him so badly that he jumps off a cliff to his death. Frye gives his terrified character an affecting vulnerability, making his doom all the more poignant. One of the villagers drives a stake through his corpse, and he and the others abandon the body in the cave. When Karl discovers that Herman was innocent, he orders the Burgermeister to give him a decent burial.

Although Frye wholeheartedly played his role, he was unhappy with it. In the film's pressbook, he proclaimed, "If God is good, I will be able to play comedy in which I was featured on Broadway for eight seasons and in which no producer of motion pictures will give me a chance! And please, God, may it be before I go screwy playing idiots, halfwits, and lunatics on the talking screen!" Ten years later, the actor got an opportunity to escape this typecasting. He was offered the role of Secretary of War Newton D. Baker in Darryl F. Zanuck's presidential biopic *Wilson*. Tragically, Frye died of a heart attack before filming began. He had been ailing for some time, but he refused to seek treatment because he was a devout Christian Scientist.

Lionel Atwill, like Dwight Frye, had distinguished himself on Broadway before he acted in horror movies. Unlike Frye, he did not find film work demeaning. He told the press, "Frankly, I've had my fill of art. It's all very well in its way, but there's an entirely different fascination to pictures that I haven't gotten over yet. No doubt I never will. It may be a little childish, but the sheer mechanical ingenuity of the whole thing gets under my skin the way a mechanical toy fascinates a boy. I've been having a tremendous good time and I don't see why I should stop."

Atwill remained active in movies until his death in 1946. His next one would be a new Technicolor shocker from Warner Brothers. Since *Doctor X* had made a bundle for the studio, Warners brought back Atwill, Fay Wray, director Michael Curtiz, and art director Anton Grot for its new thriller. *New York Times* critic Mordaunt Hall commented that *Doctor X* almost made *Frankenstein* "seem tame and friendly." Warners' new movie would surpass *Doctor X* in grisliness. Indeed, the filming would be a terrifying experience for Fay Wray.

MYSTERY OF THE WAX MUSEUM (1933)

Released on February 18, 1933 by Warner Brothers; *Director:* **Michael Curtiz;** *Producer:* **Henry Blanke;** *Screenplay:* **Don Mullaly and Carl Erickson, from a story by Charles Belden;** *Photography in two-color Technicolor process:* **Ray Rennahan;** *Editor:* **George Amy;** *Art Director:* **Anton Grot;** *Makeup by:* **Perc Westmore;** *Vitaphone Orchestra Conductor:* **Leo F. Forbstein; 79 minutes.**

Cast: **Lionel Atwill (Ivan Igor), Fay Wray (Charlotte Duncan), Glenda Farrell (Florence Dempsey), Frank McHugh (Jim, the Editor), Allen Vincent (Ralph Burton), Gavin Gordon (George Winton), Edwin Maxwell (Joe Worth), Holmes Herbert (Dr. Rasmussen), Claude King (Golatily), Arthur Edmund Carewe (Sparrow), Thomas Jackson (Detective), DeWitt Jennings (Police Captain), Matthew Betz (Otto), Monica Bannister (Joan Gale), Bull Anderson (Janitor), Pat O'Malley (Plainclothes Man).**

SYNOPSIS: In 1921 London, sculptor Ivan Igor runs a critically-acclaimed wax museum. His greedy and treacherous partner Joe Worth burns down the museum for insurance and leaves the protesting Igor to die in the flames. Twelve years later, the prematurely-aged Igor moves to New York City to open a new wax museum. The fire has damaged Igor's hands so he can no longer create wax figures. Driven mad and desperate to revive his works of art, he orders his assistants to kill people so their corpses can be used as wax figures. Igor is especially interested in Charlotte Duncan, a beautiful woman who resembles his destroyed masterpiece Marie Antoinette. Charlotte's friend, reporter Florence Dempsey, discovers the new museum's horrifying secret, and with the help of the police, saves Charlotte before Igor can make her a statue. Fighting the police, the deranged sculptor falls to his death in a vat of wax.

Warner Brothers' previous horror *Doctor X* hinted at the American city's harshness and corruption. The studio's followup, *The Mystery of the Wax Museum,* dwells on the urban underbelly. Joe Worth (Edwin Maxwell), the scoundrel responsible for the London wax museum's fire and the unhinging of Ivan Igor (Lionel Atwill), profits in New York City from the bootlegging and narcotics rackets. Sparrow (Arthur Edmund Carewe) depends on Worth for his drug habit. (The film doesn't indicate what Sparrow is addicted to, but the screenplay implies he is a cocaine fiend.) The vengeful Igor, who eventually kills Worth, not only hires Sparrow to help him steal corpses but to inform him of the arsonist's whereabouts. Police brutality is obvious; when the lawmen capture Sparrow, they subject him to the agony of withdrawal so he'll break down and spill the beans about Igor.

The city's inhabitants shrug off the environment's ordinary brutalities. When a doctor informs a reporter that Joan Gale (whose body is subsequently stolen to be used as one of Igor's wax figures) committed suicide, the newsman exults, "Gee! That'll make a swell story!" One of the morgue attendants casually explains to another how a woman died as if he was talking about the weather: "Husband slapped her full of lumps ... said she talked too much." When the woman's body rises and gasps due to the embalming fluid, the same attendant who discussed her death cracks, "Ain't that just like a woman ... always has to have the last word."

Even Florence Dempsey (Glenda Farrell), the reporter who discovers the New York City museum's ghastly secret, has a hard-boiled streak. When she learns that Joan Gale's body has been pilfered, the newswoman is initially elated; she's got a great story for her boss Jim (Frank McHugh). Jim had previously warned Florence that if she didn't stop goofing off and get a scoop, she would be out of a job. Considering the current economic crisis, Florence's euphoria is forgivable.

Dreadful as suicide and domestic violence are, they are everyday occurrences. Corpse stealing, shocking as it is, isn't that unusual. When Florence informs Jim about Joan Gale's body, he coolly tells her to look into it. Part of the horror in *Mystery of the Wax Museum* is what Ivan Igor does with the stolen corpses, coating them in wax to display in his museum. Florence initially thinks Igor's using the cadavers as models for the wax figures. And when she tells her theory to Jim, he scoffs at it: "Work that up into a comic strip and syndicate it." When Florence learns what Igor has been doing with the corpses, this revelation rattles the usually-unflappable newswoman.

Igor's passion for the cadavers he uses as wax figures smacks of necrophilia. But unlike Hjalmar Poelzig in *The Black Cat*, he has no sexual interest. Igor's attitude is paternal; he sees the corpses as the resurrections of offspring that perished in the fire. In the beginning of the film, when he shows off the original wax statues to his friends, he calls them "my children." Later in the film, when he spots Charlotte Duncan (Fay Wray), the spitting image of his destroyed figurine Marie Antoninette, he repeatedly addresses her as "my child." Igor's ardor for her is not for a sex object but for a long lost daughter. Atwill's fervor for Wray's character is appropriately menacing. But the actor eschews any kinky nuances; unlike his later portrayal in *Murders in the Zoo*, he doesn't lust for his female captive.

The horror in *Mystery of the Wax Museum* also derives from Igor's scarred and discolored visage. Perc Westmore's makeup remains effectively ghastly even today. Had *Wax Museum* been filmed in black and white, the makeup would not have looked as shocking. People with hideously-malformed faces, unlike junkies and crooks, are not a common sight in *Wax Museum*'s metropolis. Florence is so startled by Igor's burnt face that she tells the police, "He made Frankenstein look like a lily!" Less than two years after *Frankenstein*'s release, the public was already identifying the monster, rather than the doctor, with that Germanic surname. Florence's remark is also Warner Brothers' way of boasting that *Wax Museum*'s disfigured maniac is a more formidable menace than Universal's man made creature.

Glenda Farrell and the other people on the *Wax Museum* set genuinely found Atwill's makeup terrifying. "I used to sit while we were waiting our turn to go in front of the camera," the actress later recalled, "and I couldn't bear to look at him, it was so frightening. We all had nightmares about him. It was a dreadful makeup—dreadful, from the standpoint of horror."

Fay Wray was as petrified as her character when she did the first take of Igor's unmasking scene. Michael Curtiz wanted her to express genuine shock, so he didn't let her see Atwill's makeup beforehand. "I knew there was going to be an ugliness underneath," Wray remembered, "but somehow when I did it and the mask fell away I just couldn't move for a fraction of a second. I broke through it and it cracked off. Well, I had not been prepared for what I would see underneath. So when I hit him, part of it fell away. It was so—I had such revulsion. I just froze...."

The director was furious with Fay; he wanted her to keep striking Atwill until his entire mask fell apart. But Curtiz, a native Hungarian who never completely mastered the English language, didn't tell her this before the shooting. "I could have done it if I had known," Wray said, "but I would have had to shut my eyes. I couldn't have looked at his face, seeing and just kept hitting...." Luckily, an extra mask for Atwill was available. When he wore it for the reshooting, the fully prepared Fay struck him until the entire mask fell off.

Local censors had other complaints about *Mystery of the Wax Museum*. The New York state censors removed a scene where Joe Worth lights a cigar to demonstrate how to burn the London museum down. "... As if the audience needed protection from the knowledge of the various means by which a flame could be produced," David J. Skal wryly notes in his study *The Monster Show*. The Ohio Department of Film Censorship permitted *Wax Museum*'s screenings after making cuts. But B.O. Skinner, the department's director of education, hated the movie: "I wish ... to register a formal protest against the film. It contains so many elements we find objectionable, as setting fire to the museum to obtain insurance, naming a poison and telling how it could be taken to produce death, using of dope and also the general theme of horror. I feel it would be much better for all of us if the production of this type of film would be discontinued."

Skinner's diatribe was in a private correspondence with Warner Brothers. But if he had aired his screed to the press, it is unlikely he would have discouraged many people from seeing *Wax Museum*. The shocker made even more money than *Doctor X* in the United States, and it also did well overseas. But *Photoplay*'s critic warned its readers, "Don't take the kiddies." A.B. Jefferis, who ran the New Piedmont Theatre in Piedmont, Missouri, commented in *The Motion Picture Herald* that when the film was screened, "Some kids were scared and left before the show was over." Indeed, the Virginia censors recommended that nobody under the age of fourteen should see *Wax Museum* unless they were with an adult family member.

The critics were divided in judging the movie's grisliness. A collection of quotes in the "New York Reviews" section of *The Hollywood Reporter* reveals their mixed reactions. *The New York Times* critic shuddered, "The producers appear to have sought to outdo all the horror perpetuated by those old masters—Frankenstein, Dr. Moreau and the redoubtable Dr. X—and the result is too ghastly for comfort." The *Daily News* critic found *Wax Museum* entertainingly scary: "... It is sufficiently fanciful and gruesome to interest, shock and entertain." The *New York Post* found the film lacking in chills: "In spite of its intenseness [sic] on the macabre, it never achieves anything but a wax-like imitation of horror." The diversity of critical reactions to *Wax Museum* indicates that terror, like other cinematic aspects including acting and cinematography, is subjective.

Warners' publicity department marketed *Wax Museum* as first and foremost a mystery. The film's pressbook advised exhibitors, "Suspense is the keynote of your campaign on *The Mystery of the Wax Museum*, with the novelty production idea secondary but still vitally important." The term "novelty production idea" was the pressbook's euphemism for "horror;" the studio was hesitant in promoting *Wax Museum*'s bloodcurdling qualities. Studio head Jack Warner reportedly disdained the horror genre.

If the publicity department didn't want to play up *Wax Museum*'s horror elements, it had no qualms about tantalizing filmgoers with suggestive ads. Posters depicted torsos of naked, busty ladies. The artists got away with the nudity because the ladies were supposed to be *wax figures*, not *flesh and blood women*. The slogans also catered to patrons' carnal impulses. One advertisement proclaimed, "WHAT HAPPENS? With every beautiful wax model he creates, a lovely lady disappears forever!" Another advertisement displaying a full-figured female wax figure and a female wax torso described them as "IMAGES OF WAX THAT THROBBED WITH HUMAN PASSION......ALMOST WOMAN! WHAT DID THEY LACK?" These posters were misleading, since in the film Igor also uses dead men as wax statues.

Fay Wray's curvaceous assets were also exploited. One poster exhibited her posing seductively in a flimsy negligee. Lionel Atwill (not in his burnt-face makeup) also appeared in the poster looking at her approvingly. This advertisement deceptively suggested that Atwill's character lusted after Wray's character. It also marketed the actor's cinematic image as a lecher; he was typecast in that role in both horror and non-horror films. Even after the Code was strengthened, Atwill continued to play dirty old men. Ironically, the off-screen Atwill got caught up in a sex scandal in the early 1940s that tarnished his career.

Those who were lured by ads to see *Wax Museum* got the opportunity to ogle at Wray on the screen. Wray first appears in the beginning as the wax figure Marie Antoinette. (Because the wax figures quickly melted under the powerful lights used for the Technicolor two-color process, actors posed as the statues.) When we first see her as Charlotte Duncan, she is exercising in shorts. Later in the scene, while conversing with her roommate Florence, she is casually putting on her stockings. In the climax, Igor takes off all of the captive Charlotte's clothes so he can coat her in wax. Even in the pre-Code area, full nudity was forbidden on the screen, but the implication that Wray was naked must have titillated moviegoers.

Glenda Farrell's wisecracking is intended to provide filmgoers with a respite from the film's luridness. The pressbook advised exhibitors that her comical antics could "stand a heavy play if you want to appeal to the laugh fans." Her repartee is occasionally suggestive although mild by today's standards. Her remark to someone that "you can go to some nice warm place, and I don't mean California" would never be allowed in a post-Code production.

When Jim dismisses her suggestion that Ivan Igor is stealing the corpses for his wax museum, Florence starts to grumble, implying she plans to curse at him. But Jim objects, and the newswoman stops herself. The screenplay originally had her silently mouth "son of a bitch," but for obvious reasons, it wasn't filmed. Florence even has a racy bit with a policeman friend (Robert Emmett O'Connor). When she greets him at the station, she cracks, "How's your sex life?" She gets a clue when she notices he's looking at a photo of a scantily-clad woman. This segment is reminiscent of the scene in *Doctor X* where the detectives notice Dr. Haines has been perusing a book of French erotica.

Despite *Mystery of the Wax Museum*'s box office success, Warner Brothers made no more horror films during the reminder of the pre-Code era. But filmgoers would soon see Fay Wray in a new shocker. This movie would be Wray's most famous film. Filmed at RKO where she did *The Most Dangerous Game*, the actress' antagonist would be far more formidable than Ivan Igor. In reality, this creature was an eighteen-inch model covered in bear fur. But through the wonders of special effects trickery, he appeared on screen as a mighty beast, living up to his billing as the Eighth Wonder of the World.

KING KONG (1933)

Released March 2, 1933; RKO-Radio Pictures, Inc,; *Producers and Directors:* **Merian C. Cooper and Ernest B. Schoedsack;** *Executive Producer:* **David O. Selznick.;** *Screenplay:* **James A. Creelman and Ruth Rose;** *Ideas Conceived by:* **Merian C. Cooper and Edgar Wallace;** *Chief Technician:* **Willis H. O'Brien;** *Technical Staff:* **E.B. Gibson, Marcel Delgado, Fred Reefe, Orville Goldner and Carroll Shepphird;** *Art Technicians:* **Mario Larrinaga and Byron L. Crabbe;** *Photography:* **Eddie Linden and Vernon L. Walker;** *Editor:* **Ted Cheesman;** *Art Technicians:* **Mario Larrinaga and Byron L. Crabbe;** *Music:* **Max Steiner;** *Special Effects:* **Harry Redmond, Jr.;** *Associate Sound Effects:* **Walter G. Elliott;** *Makeup Supervision:* **Mel Berns; 100 minutes.**

Cast: **Fay Wray (Ann Darrow), Robert Armstrong (Carl Denham), Bruce Cabot (John Driscoll), Frank Reicher (Captain Englehorn), Sam Hardy (Charles Weston), Noble Johnson (Native Chief), Steve Clemento (Witch King), James Flavin (Second Mate Briggs), Victor Wong (Charley), Paul Porcasi (Socrates), Russ Powell (Dock Watchman).**

SYNOPSIS: Film producer Carl Denham leads a crew on a voyage to the uncharted Skull Island in the South Seas to make an adventure film. A down and out woman named Ann Darrow gratefully accepts his offer to star in the film. When Denham, Darrow, and the others land on Skull Island, they discover the natives in the middle of a ceremony sacrificing one of their women to the giant ape Kong. The natives abduct Darrow to use her as the next sacrifice, but the ape falls in love with the lovely, terrified woman. She is rescued by first mate Jack Driscoll. Denham and his crew subdue Kong and take the primate to New York City to exhibit him in chains as "The Eighth Wonder of the World."

Kong escapes, recaptures Darrow, and carries her to the top of the Empire State Building. Men in airplanes shoot at Kong. Just before he falls to his death on New York's streets, the primate gently places Darrow down on a rooftop.

Murders in the Rue Morgue's perverse concept of an ape's passion for a human woman is revived and enhanced in *King Kong*. Erik the ape's behavior in *Rue Morgue* seems proper compared to Kong's. Erik just grabs Camille and runs off with her. Kong fondles Ann Darrow (Fay Wray) and removes the terrified girl's garments. If Kong was depicted as a normal-sized primate, the Production Code would have probably not allowed him to paw at Ann. But Kong is a gigantic primate who carries Ann like a doll; it is impossible for him to have relations with her. Besides, he is a fantastic creature like Dracula and Imhotep. Forty-foot gorillas don't exist and never have.

Merian C. Cooper, who conceived the fantastic *King Kong* concept, vehemently denied the stripping scene had any prurient overtones. In a letter to a fan many years after the film's initial release, he contended, "I played this scene as a great gorilla playing as with a toy—and played it for comedy—and so the 1933 audiences took it . . . It had *no* decadent 'rape' concept or execution!!!" Had Depression-era viewers been offended by this scene, it would have hurt *Kong*'s box office prospects. But Ann Darrow isn't amused when the ape takes off her clothes. Her terrified expression indicates she feels violated. The stripping scene is simultaneously humorous and horrifying.

The stripping scene also wouldn't have been permitted under the strengthened Production Code. When *King Kong* was rereleased in 1938, the censors deleted this segment. They also scissored out the film's more grisly aspects, particularly the primate's chewing on a New Yorker and dropping a city woman to her death. The censors were also offended by the film's gory bits—blood spurting from a slain tyrannosaur's jaw and a gaping bullet wound on Kong's chest. New prints were issued that were more darkly photographed than the originals so the bloodshed was less visible. The eliminated segments wouldn't reappear in subsequent reissues for over thirty years. In 1967, a private film collector learned that a former projectionist had stashed the missing footage. In 1970, a fully restored *King Kong* print was issued in theaters. Curiously, the post-1934 Production Code version of *King Kong* retained a momentary scene of Fay Wray's exposed breast. She escapes the ape's clutches on Skull Island by jumping into a lake. When Fay emerges, one of her bosoms pops out of her blouse. Either the censors didn't notice or they believed that audiences wouldn't.

King Kong got into trouble with local censors during its initial showing in 1933. New York's censorship board deleted the stripping segment and scenes of Kong stepping on and biting people before allowing it to be screened there. (These censors didn't spot Wray's bared breast.) RKO actually eliminated a frightening scene from the film before its release. It was supposed to follow the segment where Kong shakes a tree bridge on Skull Island, causing many crewmen to plummet. As originally filmed, the men landed in a valley where giant spiders and lizards devoured them. For years, a rumor circulated that the crewmen's gruesome fate so upset preview audiences they couldn't concentrate on the rest of the film. In fact, the spiders and lizards segment was eliminated before previews. "It ... just stopped the picture cold," Cooper told film scholar Kevin Brownlow. "It broke every rule ... about picture making ... Our whole thesis ... is to start a picture slow and get everybody to know the characters and to get the feel of what we're going to tell. And once you start moving, never let it stop, just drive it on."

The Production Code did intervene during the film's production. Scenarist Ruth Rose had invented a language for the Skull Island natives. She didn't create it entirely from her imagination; it was derived from an actual language in Palau Nias, an island in the Indian Ocean west of Sumatra. The Code worried that Rose would give the islanders coarse dialogue, so the censors insisted that Rose provide an English translation! She complied and the Code found nothing objectionable. The Code wasn't concerned about the sensitivities of the Nias Islanders; there was no market for *Kong* screenings there.

Whatever problems *King Kong* had with the censors, they did not interfere with its box office success. Filmgoers found the action on screen thrilling. Mordaunt Hall in his *New York Times* review reported, "... this picture was received by many a giggle to cover up fright. Constant exclamations issued ... 'What a man!' observed one youth when the ape forced down the great oaken door on the island." If the public was frightened by Kong, they were also impressed. The great ape was oddly attractive, like his predecessors Dracula and the Frankenstein Monster.

Modern Screen recommended *King Kong* for all ages: "Very good—children will be thrilled." In fact, the youngsters' reactions varied. A.B. Jefferis, who managed the New Piedmont Theatre in Piedmont, Missouri, reported to *The Motion Picture Herald* that even though the patrons enjoyed the film, "many of the kids were scared." P.G. Estes, who ran the S.T. Theatre in Parker, South Dakota, told the same publication, "The youngsters were in most cases too busy figuring how ... [the special effects of Kong and the other monsters] . . . could be done to be very scared." As noted in an earlier chapter on *Mystery of the Wax Museum*, cinematic terror is subjective. What frightens some children intrigues others. P.G. Estes' commentary indicates that a lot of Depression-era youngsters recognized that King Kong was make believe. The film's promoters didn't want to only attract children. They played up Fay Wray's attributes. Posters and lobby cards depicted Kong clutching a skimpily-clad and leggy Wray. Some advertisements prominently displayed photos of a frightened looking Wray in her ripped garments. Fay's petrified poses stressed *Kong*'s horror and sex elements. She recognized the torn clothing's publicity value. On one occasion, she dressed like that for a real-life costume party which was filmed for a short subject in Paramount's *Hollywood on Parade* series. These shorts depicted film performers' comical off-screen antics. (Bela Lugosi appeared in another short as Dracula terrorizing an actress dressed as Betty Boop.)

The public eagerly responded to the advertisements. To them, *King Kong* was a welcome diversion from the nation's economic troubles. But this film, more than any of the other pre-Code horrors, deals with the Great Depression. When Carl Denham (Robert Armstrong) looks for a leading lady in New York City for his upcoming picture, he sees women standing in the breadlines. While Denham chats with the grocery vendor Socrates (Paul Porcasi), Ann Darrow furtively attempts to steal an apple. Looking fatigued and shabbily dressed, she seems a typical victim of the Depression.

She is obviously penniless; when Socrates threatens to have her arrested, Denham pays for the apple. Ann then faints in Carl's arms; she is starving.

After treating her to a meal, Denham offers her the role in his new picture. At first, Ann misunderstands his promise of "money, adventure, and fame." She stammers, "No! Wait, I can't—I don't understand—you must tell me—I do want the job so—I was starving—but I can't...." Denham assures her, "This is strictly business. I'm no chaser." Incredibly, this suggestive dialogue exchange was not removed in post-Code *Kong* screenings. But the scene sheds light on the real-life desperation of struggling American women in 1933.

Most of what follows in *King Kong* is escapist fantasy. Skull Island is an enthralling if unsettling place with fantastic creatures. The spectacle of Kong wrecking havoc in New York City may have temporarily frightened viewers, but it took them away from harsh reality.

The filmmakers didn't make Kong too horrifying. The creature wasn't consciously evil like Dracula and Dr. Moreau; he was just a wild animal acting on his instincts. When Kong falls off the Empire State Building, after gently placing Ann down, Max Steiner's score becomes melancholy in tone. And when Carl Denham views the ape's corpse and says the immortal closing line, "It was beauty killed the beast," he looks and sounds regretful. One critic acknowledged Kong's tragic qualities. *The Hollywood Reporter*'s reviewer wrote, "Even though he kills off anything and everything that seeks to intrude on his romance with the beauty, when he is finally killed ...you almost have to choke down a tear for his passing."

King Kong was actually an eighteen-inch model covered in bear fur. Thanks to RKO's special effects department, particularly Willis H. O'Brien's stop-motion animation, the gorilla was a believable menace on screen. But the model wasn't used for all of Kong's scenes. A giant head, arm and hand, and foot were used for the ape's close-ups. A film crew worker would place the hand's flexible fingers around Fay Wray's waist for her scenes in Kong's hand. For the arm to move, it was attached to a lever. Wray found being in the ape's hand even scarier than Lionel Atwill's burnt makeup in *Mystery of the Wax Museum*; she feared that she would slip and fall from the contraption. She later said her frightened expression in the filmed hand scenes was real.

Having survived *Kong*'s filming, Wray considered the finished product a mixed blessing. She was impressed with the film and its box office success. But just as her *Vampire Bat* co-star Dwight Frye found himself typecast as either a lunatic or a half-wit, Fay was deluged with film offers as a damsel in distress. She had already proven herself a distinguished serious actress, particularly in Erich von Stroheim's silent drama *The Wedding March*. Wray so dreaded the prospect of being pigeonholed as a scream queen that she temporarily escaped Hollywood to work in Great Britain. Eventually, Wray made peace with her *King Kong* association. She even titled her autobiography *On the Other Hand*. On August 12, 2004, two days after Wray passed away, the Empire State Building's lights were dimmed for fifteen minutes in her honor.

In the same month that RKO released *King Kong*, Paramount issued a new horror film, *Murders in the Zoo*. Unlike *Kong*'s titular creature, *Zoo*'s big terror was a human being: Wray's former co-star Lionel Atwill. But like *Kong*, Paramount's shocker featured beasts battling each other. But Paramount avoided special effects work; these animals were real. In retrospect, *Zoo*'s crew would have fared better with special effects; the filming of the fighting animals resulted in a catastrophe that outraged animal rights activists and damaged the movie's public reputation.

MURDERS IN THE ZOO (1933)

Released March 31, 1933 by Paramount; *Director:* **Edward Sutherland;** *Associate Producer:* **E. Lloyd Sheldon;** *Screenplay:* **Philip Wylie and Seton I. Miller;** *Additional Dialogue:* **Milton H. Gropper;** *Director of Photography:* **Ernest Haller; 61 minutes.**

Cast: **Charlie Ruggles (Peter Yates), Lionel Atwill (Eric Gorman), Gail Patrick (Jerry Evans), Randolph Scott (Dr. Woodford), John Lodge (Roger Hewitt), Kathleen Burke (Evelyn Gorman), Harry Beresford (Professor Evans), Edward McWade (Dan).**

SYNOPSIS: Wealthy zoologist Eric Gorman murders men he believes are fooling around with his wife Evelyn. When he learns that she is having an affair with Roger Hewitt, Gorman arranges a fundraising banquet at his zoo. There, Roger is fatally bitten by a mamba, a venomous snake. When Evelyn learns of this and tells her husband she will turn him in to the law, Eric throws her in the alligator pound, where she is devoured. He feigns innocence, but Dr. Woodford, who works at the zoo, learns the truth and informs the police. Fleeing the lawmen, Gorman frees his big cats from their cages. One of the beasts chases him into a boa constrictor's cage, where the creature strangles him to death.

Of all the pre-Code Hollywood horrors, *Murders in the Zoo* must have been the most unsettling for contemporary American filmgoers. Most of the film's terrors don't occur in a faraway place like a tropical island or Continental Europe but in the American streets. Director Edward Sutherland deliberately avoids Gothic trappings to present a realistic urban milieu. As for the film's villain, Eric Gorman, he must have disturbed audiences more than any of the terror genre's previous fiends and monsters. He isn't a make-believe character like the vampire Dracula and the mummy Imhotep. Nor is he a wronged soul entitled to some sympathy like the titular *Freaks* and Ivan Igor. Gorman isn't even trying to make a scientific point like the mad doctors Mirakle and Moreau. He is a degenerate who gleefully murders men he believes his wife has romanced, a sadist who torments his unfortunate spouse. People like Eric Gorman actually existed; even filmgoers who didn't personally know such criminals read about them in the newspapers.

Lionel Atwill's performance as Gorman enhances the character's vileness. As William K. Everson points out in *Classics of the Horror Film*, the actor "managed to suggest general tendencies toward unspecified depravities which [the script] never intended. The gleam that came into Atwill's eye, the sneer of his lips, his quick dismissal of unspeakable things that had happened off-screen before the story got under way, all of these little acting ploys somehow turned him into an unwholesome killer as well as an illegal one!"

Either Boris Karloff or Bela Lugosi could have been wickedly charismatic as Gorman. But neither actor would have imbued the role with such kinky nuances. Perhaps they feared that if they utilized them, they would repulse, rather than merely frighten, audiences. Atwill had no such compunctions; he reveled in his twisted on-screen persona. He told a reporter for *Motion Picture Magazine*, "See, one side of my face is gentle and kind, incapable of anything but love of my fellow man. The other side, the other profile, is cruel and predatory and evil, incapable of anything but the lusts and dark passions. *It all depends on which side of my face is turned toward you—or the camera.* It all depends on which side faces the moon at the ebb of the tide."

In his younger days, Atwill had been a matinee idol on the stage. By the time he arrived in Hollywood in the early 1930s, he was middle-aged and portly. Nevertheless, his profile, particularly his hypnotic eyes, was still debonair and dashing. *Motion Picture Magazine* played up both Atwill's allure and horror: "Here is a *handsome* man who makes women's hearts beat faster—*until he stops them.* Here is a charming and very polished gentleman who makes women's blood run warmer—*until he chills it.*" Older female (and closeted gay) filmgoers with memories of Lionel's earlier theater work may have been both aroused and repelled by Atwill's Eric Gorman.

Murders in the Zoo's opening scene remains as shocking today as it was back in 1933. In a jungle clearing, a man is pinned on the ground by two natives. Gorman bends over the captive, stitching something. As he sews, Eric proclaims, "A Mongolian prince taught me this, Taylor. An ingenious device for the right occasion. You'll never lie to a friend again and you'll never kiss another man's wife."

When he completes his task, Gorman and his natives depart. Taylor, his hands tied behind his back, gets to his feet and staggers off into the jungle. Director Sutherland then provides a shot of Gorman leaving astride an elephant. Once Eric has gone, Taylor reappears, stumbling forward until his face is in close-up. We see *what* Gorman had been sewing—the unfortunate man's lips are literally sealed! What's horrific about this sight is not only the stitched and bloodied mouth but his pained and terrified eyes. We are not only repulsed by the hideous sight but by the perpetuator's cruelty.

This grisly scene has a darkly-humorous follow-up. When Gorman returns to his compound, his wife Evelyn (Kathleen Burke, *Island of Lost Souls*'s Panther Woman) asks him about Taylor. Gorman tells her he has departed. When Evelyn asks him what Taylor said before leaving, Eric nonchalantly replies, "He didn't say anything." Had Sutherland not graphically depicted Taylor's disfigurement, the chilling double meaning in Gorman's remark would not have come across so strongly.

None of the subsequent shock elements in *Murders* are as graphic as the opening scene. The filmmakers must have realized that it was impossible to devise anything that would surpass the luridness of Taylor's sewn up mouth. Even though the Production Code wasn't enforced, the censors still would have objected to an overload of gore. But due to Sutherland's skillful direction, the horror remains strong.

Especially frightening is the climax where the big cats are let loose and start attacking each other. The sight of lions fighting leopards and panthers fighting pumas is even more disturbing than the sight of Taylor's stitched lips. Gorman's macabre needlework is just makeup, but the feline-to-feline combat is real. Paramount publicized the filming of the battle, inviting its stars (including *Dr.*

Jekyll and Mr. Hyde's tragic siren Miriam Hopkins) and the press to view it from a platform above the arena. The guests were protected from the animals by heavy wire fencing. The studio also invited representatives from the American Society for the Prevention of Cruelty to Animals (ASPCA) to assure them that the big cats were humanely handled.

To say that the publicity stunt was a disaster would be an understatement. As the animals, freed from an enclosure, fought each other, some spectators screamed and fainted while others ran for cover. One lion ripped the neck of a lioness. Another lion severely mauled a puma. The puma was so badly injured that trainers gave it a mercy killing. A leopard escaped through the wire screen. One of the trainers discovered the big cat hiding under a pile of banks. Four hours passed before the trainers successfully rounded up the hyperactive beasts and corralled them back into their cages. Yet Paramount successfully filmed the animal mayhem and utilized it in the film. But the studio could not prevent the press from trumpeting the mayhem's gruesome results. Alarmed about *Murders in the Zoo*'s box office prospects, Paramount hoped the zoological bloodbath would boost the film's horror angle, attracting the morbidly interested. The publicity may have drawn these patrons but not enough to make *Murders in the Zoo* a smash.

What's even more frightening than Gorman's crimes per se is the perverse thrill he gets out of them. His atrocities induce amorous feelings for his wife. This is particularly evident after Eric disposes of Roger Hewitt (John Lodge). Leering at Evelyn, Gorman grabs her and strokes her hair, his hand nearly touching her breast twice. Evelyn is repulsed ("Don't touch me!"), but her protests only heighten Eric's ardor: "I'm not going to kiss you. *You're* going to kiss *me!*" Not since *Dr. Jekyll and Mr. Hyde* has sexual harassment been brazenly depicted in a pre-Code horror. Gorman's behavior is even scarier than his predecessor's. The simian-looking Hyde is a fantasy figure, the outward manifestation of Jekyll's dark side. Gorman is an ordinary-looking human, someone who actually exists.

Paramount knew that Lionel Atwill was an effective villain, but the studio was worried that *Murders in the Zoo* would trouble filmgoers if the film concentrated entirely on his wickedness. Unlike the studio's previous horrors, *Dr. Jekyll and Mr. Hyde* and *Island of Lost Souls*, this film provided comic relief in the timorous character of Peter Yates. Charlie Ruggles, who played Yates, was a popular film comedian. He also provided humorous diversion in the studio's murder melodrama *Terror Aboard*, also released in 1933. Ruggles was even given top billing in *Murders*. William K. Everson in *Classics of the Horror Film* speculates that he was billed above Atwill because he was a Paramount contract player, whereas Atwill was a freelancer. But the studio may have also used Ruggles's name at the head of the cast to assure box office patrons that despite the title, *Murders in the Zoo* would offer them lighthearted laughs to offset its horrors.

Not all of the film's goofy humor, however, would be accepted by the soon to be enforced Production Code. In one scene where Yates is cleaning a cage, he discovers the missing mamba Gorman used to kill Roger Hewitt. Yates faints, and when he comes to, he nervously says, "Is there a good laundry in this town?" Yates' embarrassing alcoholic past is also played for laughs. When he falls off the wagon and no longer fears the animals at the film's end, his drunkeness is supposed to be funny. Curiously, when the Code was strengthened, it continued to permit comical inebriation on screen. Depression-era society was not as aware of alcohol's detrimental effects as today's society.

Despite Ruggles' presence, Paramount's publicity department exploited the film's lurid aspects. One ad proclaimed, "HE SEWED A MAN'S LIPS TOGETHER . . . For Daring to Look at Her with Eyes of Love!" It had a photograph of an enraged-looking Atwill dragging a terrified looking Burke by her wrists across the floor. This ad, unlike the film itself, actually gives Atwill top billing. Other promos gave Ruggles top billing but emphasized the film's horrors with Lionel's chilling visage. These ads also reminded patrons of Burke's previous role in *Island of Lost Souls* by inserting "The Panther Woman" in parentheses under her name.

All the ballyhoo could not ensure *Murders in the Zoo*'s box office success. It wasn't a flop, but the film didn't do as much business as Paramount hoped. Two exhibitor reports to the *Motion Picture Herald* reveal the public's mixed reactions. W.H. Brenner of the Cozy Theatre of Winchester, Indiana wrote that he "had the biggest Sunday business in three months. The picture deals with wild animals and science in an interesting and entertaining manner." R.W. Hickman of the Lyric Theatre of Greenville, Illinois, however, found patrons unsatisfied with the film and cautioned other exhibitors, "Most likely you'll starve to death with it. Don't believe that it will please a living soul. Too bad they continue to make this type of picture."

Was *Murders in the Zoo* too horrifying for many Depression-era filmgoers to enjoy it? Perhaps, even if the press hadn't reported about the abused animals. *The Los Angeles Examiner* wrote at the film's Hollywood premiere, "Roars, shrieks, and cacklings of the wild animals on the screen at the Paramount Theatre yesterday were echoed to an amazing degree by the audience, at times driven to a mild state of hysteria by scenes of *Murders in the Zoo*...." Andre Sennwald, reviewing the film for the *New York Times*, contended, "It happens that the director has been almost too effective in dramatizing ... cheerless events ... Lionel Atwill as the insanely jealous husband is almost too convincing for comfort...." It's likely that many box office patrons agreed with him. Some of them, however, may have been morbidly fascinated *because* Atwill was almost too convincing for comfort. That may have been one reason why it did well in Winchester, Indiana.

Even if *Murders in the Zoo*'s shocks weren't blatant, and even if Atwill's villainy lacked lewd insinuations, the film might still not have been a big hit. Norbert Lusk, who liked *Murders in the Zoo*, pointed out in the *Los Angeles Times*, "The cast is not strong in box office names and because of this it may never achieve the success it deserves...." Atwill and Charlie Ruggles enjoyed steady film work, but mainly as character actors. Neither of them became stars of the first magnitude. Romantic lead Randolph Scott was not yet a big star.

Nevertheless, after the Production Code was strengthened, Paramount was able to reissue the film. Of course, the studio's publicity department could exploit Scott's role in rereleases. But although censor Joseph Breen gave the film a Reissue Code seal, he did so with two caveats: "Eliminate close-up of man's lips stitched together ... Eliminate line: 'Is there a good laundry in this town?'" But with censorship rules relaxed today, *Murders in the Zoo* is now available on DVD in its original pre-Code cut.

William K. Everson wrote in 1974, "In comparison with the physically repellent obsession with gore and clinical detail that has marked recent horror films, *Murders in the Zoo* seems a model of decorum. . . ." As for Charlie Ruggles' line about a good laundry, it is far less objectionable than modern movies' gross-out stunts that pass off as humor. But Atwill's performance as the depraved Eric Gorman remains profoundly disturbing. At the same time, it is oddly fascinating, thanks to the actor's colorful personality and elegant delivery. It is a testimony to Atwill's talent that even though his character is an utter reprobate devoid of any redeeming qualities, he compels our attention.

Back in 1933, when *Murders in the Zoo* was completed, Paramount planned another horror film with shocks and sex. Once again, Randolph Scott would play the male romantic lead. His girlfriend would be a woman possessed by the spirit of an executed murderer. The actress playing the role, like Scott, was a rising star. But had Paramount known what kind of star she would be, the studio wouldn't have cast her in this film. Like Myrna Loy in *The Mask of Fu Manchu*, she would distinguish herself as a comedienne. Her name was Carole Lombard.

SUPERNATURAL [1933]

Released on April 21, 1933 by Paramount; *Director:* **Victor Halperin;** *Producer:* **Edward Halperin;** *Screenplay:* **Harvey Thew and Brian Marlow, based on the story and adaptation by Garnett Weston;** *Dialogue Direction:* **Sidney Salkow;** *Photographer:* **Arthur Martinelli; 65 minutes.**

Cast: **Carole Lombard (Roma Courtney), Alan Dinehart (Paul Bavian), Vivienne Osbourne (Ruth Rogen), Randolph Scott (Grant Wilson), H.B. Warner (Dr. Houston), Beryl Mercer (Madame Gourjan), William Farnum (Robert Hammond), Willard Robertson (Warden), George Burr MacAnnon (Max), Lyman Williams (John Courtney).**

SYNOPSIS: *In New York City, Ruth Rogen is executed for killing three of her lovers. Before her electrocution, she gives scientist Dr. Houston permission to experiment on her corpse. Dr. Houston believes that an evil spirit can leave a dead body and pass on to a living being. His theory is proven correct when Ruth's spirit enters the body of Roma Courtney, who is in mourning over her recently-deceased brother John. The possessed Roma seduces quack spiritualist Paul Bavian, who ratted on Ruth to the police. Dr. Houston and Ruth's boyfriend Grant Wilson realize that Ruth's spirit is controlling Roma. With the help of John's spirit, they track Roma down before she can kill Paul. Ruth's spirit leaves Roma's body to drive Paul to his death. Roma is her sweet self again, and she and Grant plan to get married.*

Carole Lombard is best known as the daffy heroine of such zany romps as *My Man Godfrey* and *Nothing Sacred*. Why would Paramount cast her as a woman possessed by an executed murderess's soul? At the time the studio assigned her this role, she was just a budding actress who had not yet developed her breezy persona. Another year would pass before she proved her comedic chops in *Twentieth Century*.

Lombard's vehicles tended to be gritty dramas that took advantage of the lax Production Code. For instance, in *Virtue* (1932), Carole plays a former prostitute who is wrongly accused of murder. In *White Woman*, released the same year as *Supernatural*, she's a scandal-ridden nightclub singer forced to marry a sadistic jungle plantation owner (Charles Laughton in a role reminiscent of *The Island of Lost Souls*'s Dr. Moreau) to avoid deportation from Malaysia. Although Lombard's characters in these films ultimately found salvation, they endured turmoil and torment before they could enjoy their happy endings. Had Lombard established herself as a comedienne before *Supernatural* was filmed, she wouldn't have been cast in the production. That would have suited her fine; she hated the script ("Who do you have to screw to get off this picture?"), and she hated director Victor Halperin ("This guy ought to be running a deli.").

Lombard was particularly incensed at Halperin because he often placed her on the wrong side of the camera, exposing her less attractive profile. What made this profile a liability was a scar, the result of a car accident several years ago. But if Halperin had trouble remembering Carole's good profile, he did shrewdly exploit her voluptuous qualities. As Roma Courtney, Lombard is always fully dressed, but she always looks stunning. When Ruth Rogen's spirit takes over Roma's body, the blonde actress, formerly subdued, acquires a sinister expression that is both seductive and threatening. Halperin's close-ups of Lombard's menacing eyes, reminiscent of his earlier close-ups of Lugosi's eyes in his previous vehicle *White Zombie*, project a macabre sensuality.

The possessed Roma arouses Paul Bavian (Alan Dinehart), and we believe it. Filmgoers undoubtedly were aroused as well. When Bavian embraces the blonde on a sofa he places his hand on her bosom. Such a brazen action would never be allowed once the Production Code was enforced the following year. When Roma starts to strangle him, she declares, "I'm gonna kill you before I leave this body you like so much." This suggestive line also would not have been permitted had *Supernatural* been made in the post-Code era.

This remark could also have been Paramount's sly way of ballyhooing Lombard's sex appeal.

Supernatural also plays up Vivienne Osbourne's pulchritude. The newspaper clipping about her character Ruth Rogen establishes her as a sex murderer. She's a distaff version of Lionel Atwill's Eric Gorman in Paramount's previous chiller *Murders in the Zoo*. The heading proclaims "Rogen Kills Men Who Loved Her." The text underneath the heading salaciously reports, "Ruth Rogen yesterday confessed she killed each of her three lovers after a riotous orgy in her sensuous Greenwich Village apartment." The newspaper displays a photo of Rogen posing vampishly.

A kaleidoscopic montage of images following the news clipping covers Rogen's trial, including jury shots, an operating printing press, and the accused killer herself. In one of Osbourne's images, she boasts of her crimes, "I'd do it again and again and again." Reynold Humphries points out in *The Hollywood Horror Film 1931-1941*, "In the context, this means she would kill other men after more orgies if she had the chance, but the insistence on some link between sex and murder allows us to interpret the remark as a compulsive desire to have sex, thus representing Rogen as a nymphomaniac."

Another brief shot of Rogen is in her cell awaiting her execution. She wails over Paul Bavian repeatedly, "Why doesn't he come?" The statement explicitly means Ruth hopes that Paul, who turned her in to the authorities, will tell them to have her life spared. But Ruth's words could also subconsciously reveal her desire to seduce him. Indeed, when her spirit inhabits Roma's body, she proceeds to do that. We never see the possessed Roma and the infatuated Paul engage in sexual relations. But consider that Halperin fades out on the scene where they embrace on the sofa. Following a scene where Roma's boyfriend Grant Wilson (Randolph Scott) and Dr. Houston (H.B. Warner) try to find her, the camera returns to Roma and Paul, still on the sofa.

With her regal profile and feline eyes, Vivienne Osbourne looks the picture of a femme fatale. The actress tended to be cast as a bad girl in films, although none of her characters were homicidal like Ruth Rogen. Carole Lombard, on the other hand, was already a leading lady by the time *Supernatural* was made. Despite being possessed by a murderess' soul, the film did not permit her to kill Paul Bavian. Rogen's spirit leaves Roma's body to commit the crime. The Production Code may not have been enforceable, but the filmmakers could not let Lombard's character off the hook to enjoy wedded bliss with Grant Wilson if she actually took a life.

Curiously, the fate of Rogen's soul is unresolved. Has she decided to permanently depart the earth now that she has avenged Bavian? Or is she still roaming the planet, gleefully planning future murders? Had *Supernatural* been made after the Code was strengthened, the Halperins and their crew would have been told to punish Rogen's spirit. Or perhaps, she wouldn't succeed in taking Bavian's life because the frightened man would confess his crimes and surrender to the police. The film's ending, with Roma and Grant in a romantic embrace, is supposed to be uplifting. But countless horror films in the last thirty-five years have ended with the killer's disappearance, implying the fiend may return. Although the filmmakers never intended this, they pioneered this ominous theme in *Supernatural*.

This movie depicts the killings with restraint. Paul Bavian's strangulation is exhibited in a long shot and is darkly lit, obscuring his tortured facial features. Bavian's own murders, with a toxic dart in his ring puncturing his victims' hands, are virtually bloodless. When he pierces his first victim, she observes, "It's only a scratch" before realizing she's been poisoned. Nevertheless, the *Harrison's Reports* reviewer cringed, "It is . . . horrible to watch Allan [sic] Dinehart murder both a woman and a man by inserting a deadly poison into their bodies by means of a ring." Presumably, if Dinehart's character had used a conventional killing method like shooting, the reviewer would not have been too upset.

Paramount played up *Supernatural*'s mystical motif. The studio's publicity department claimed, "Followers of spiritualism throughout the world deluged Edward and Victor Halperin . . . with advice and comment when they announced plans for production of 'Supernatural.'" The pressbook alleged a woman sent the Halperins a script, contending she wrote it while under spirit control. After reading it, Edward sent it back with the following note: "Have this produced and distributed 'under spirit control.' It will be easier for all concerned."

The publicity department claimed that some spiritualists eagerly anticipated *Supernatural*'s release. They offered advice for the production and even sent invitations to attend séances and demonstrations. Other spiritualists protested the film. According to the publicity department, "Not a day passed without the arrival of a flood of telegrams, letters and other messages from 'cranks,' manly of whom delivered thinly veiled threats." One particularly threatening letter from someone called "Occulta" was quoted: "There's nothing more dangerous to human progress than misleading information pertaining to supernatural phenomena. Watch your step, or else—."

Critics found *Supernatural*'s otherworldly chills too hokey to be effective. *The Motion Picture Herald* commented, "The too obvious effort to appear mystical, mysterious and weird causes [the film] at times to descend of its own weight to something approaching absurdity." *Variety* opined, "The villain is a phony spiritualist, and he's painted with a pretty broad brush all the way. On the other hand there's a prominent scientist whose ideas are equally far-fetched ... But audiences won't believe in the scientist any more than the spiritualist, and that's 'Supernatural's' weakness." *Supernatural* fizzled at the box office. There's no definite explanation *why* the film didn't do well. Perhaps some filmgoers agreed with *Variety* that the horrors were unconvincing, or maybe other filmgoers found the horrors *too* convincing for comfort. Indeed, *Supernatural* did not escape civic condemnation.

The March 31, 1934 issue of *The Motion Picture Herald* published an analysis by Mrs. Thomas G. Winter, Hollywood's official representative of the women's organizations that previewed pictures. She declared that 13 percent of the films seen by her office in the previous year were unsuitable for public viewing. *Supernatural* was one them, with a brief comment: "Gruesome; poorly done." (*Mystery of the Wax Museum* was another horror film on her list, with the complaint: "Gruesome thriller." Curiously, neither *Island of Lost Souls* nor *Murders in the Zoo* was deemed unfit for filmgoers.)

Paramount dropped the Halperins. Although the brothers made a few more horror pictures in the post-Code era, they never worked for a major studio again. Paramount stayed away from full-fledged shockers until the end of the decade. But Universal worked on a new horror film for the fall of 1933. Once again, James Whale would direct it. Like *Island of Lost Souls*, this movie would be based on an H.G. Wells novel, *The Invisible Man*. But the renowned author would give this production his blessing. Unlike *Island of Lost Souls*, *The Invisible Man* would make a profit. And although its titular character was even more dangerous than *Supernatural*'s Ruth Rogen, the movie would avoid major censure.

THE INVISIBLE MAN [1933]

Released November 13, 1933; A Universal Picture; *Director:* **James Whale;** *Producer:* **Carl Laemmle, Jr.;** *Screenplay:* **R.C. Sherriff,** *based on H.G. Wells's novel; Photography:* **Arthur Edeson;** *Art Director:* **Charles D. Hall;** *Editor:* **Ted Kent;** *Special Effects Photography:* **John P. Fulton;** *Retake Photography and Miniatures:* **John J. Mescall;** *Visual Effects Supervisor:* **Frank D. Williams;** *Music:* **W. Franke Harling and Heinz Roemheld;** *Makeup:* **Jack P. Pierce; 70 minutes.**

Cast: **Claude Rains (Dr. Jack Griffin), Gloria Stuart (Flora Cranley), William Harrigan (Dr. Arthur Kemp), Henry Travers (Dr. Cranley), Una O'Connor (Jenny Hall), Forrester Harvey (Herbert Hall), Holmes Herbert (Chief of Police), E.E. Clive (Police Constable Jaffers), Dudley Digges (Chief of Detectives), Harry Stubbs (Police Inspector Bird), Donald Stuart (Inspector Lane), Merle Tottenham (Milly).**

SYNOPSIS: *A mysterious character whose facial features are concealed by bandages arrives at the Lion's Head Inn in the English country village of Iping one snowy evening. This character is Dr. Jack Griffin, a chemist who has made himself invisible with his own devised formula. At the inn, the secluded Griffin works in his room on a drug to make himself visible again. Unbeknownst to him, the invisibility concoction is affecting his sanity. Unable to continue work on the antidote, the maddened Griffin exposes his invisibility to the villagers and wreaks havoc in Iping. Determining to use his invisibility to take over the world, he forces his scientific colleague Dr. Arthur Kemp to become his partner. When Griffin's distraught girlfriend Flora Cranley learns the invisible man is at Kemp's, she goes there and unsuccessfully tries to persuade him to abandon his megalomaniacal schemes. While Griffin sleeps at Kemp's house, Kemp informs the police.*

Learning that Kemp has betrayed him, Griffin vows to kill him. Although the police try to protect Kemp, Griffin tracks him down. He ties Kemp up in a car and drives it off a cliff, where the vehicle explodes. The invisible man goes on a reign of terror, frustrating the police. One snowy night, he takes refuge in a barn. The farmer hears Griffin's snoring and alerts the police. Setting fire to the barn, the lawmen force Griffin out into the snow, his footprints exposed. The chief of the detectives shoots him, and when Griffin dies, he becomes visible again.

By the standards of pre-Code Hollywood, *The Invisible Man* is a tame chiller. This doesn't mean that it's tepid and dull; indeed, the invisible Jack Griffin is the most dangerous of all of pre-Code horror's monsters. He singlehandedly kills over a hundred people by derailing a train. Even King Kong, for all his immense size and strength, doesn't take so many lives at once. And unlike the giant ape, the invisible man is cunning, a greater threat to society. But in viewing *The Invisible Man*, one recognizes that unlike other shockers like *Murders in the Rue Morgue*, *Freaks*, and *Island of Lost Souls*, this film would have passed the post-1934 Code's guidelines without undergoing any major revisions.

The film's violence is suggested rather than blatant. Griffin's murder of a police inspector (Harry Stubbs) is shocking, but it's because the lawman is helpless; there is no gore like in *Murders in the Zoo*. None of the invisible man's victims are physically mutilated like the trapeze artist Cleopatra in *Freaks*. Indeed, footage of two of Griffin's crimes was reused in Universal's post-Code films. The train crash scene shows up in *Sherlock Holmes and the Voice of Terror* (1942). Dr. Kemp's exploding car appears in *The House of Fear* and *The Jungle Captive*, both released in 1945.

Griffin does, however, commit one assault that might not have been permitted in the post-Code era; he turns over a baby carriage. Presumably, the child survives; the audience is never told otherwise. Nevertheless, the very sight of an upturned baby carriage is as horrifying to the viewers as it is to the baby's mother in the film.

The invisible man may be a remorseless killer, but he is no sex maniac like Mr. Hyde or Eric Gorman. He does have amorous feelings toward Flora Cranley (Gloria Stuart), but they are tender and courtly. Indeed, Griffin's love for Flora is the last vestige of his sanity, his Dr. Jekyll aspect. But Griffin makes one suggestive remark when he takes off his clothes in the inn. Unzipping his fly, he comments, "This will give them [the villagers] a bit of a shock!" Any more provocative stunts would have been pointless. The pranks Griffin plays on bystanders and lawmen are sufficiently outrageous. John P. Fulton's special effects—a bicycle being stolen, an old man's hat thrown into a pond, etc.—are so amazing to watch that they don't have to be risqué. And if Griffin used his invisibility to chase women, it would have trivialized the film's tragic romantic aspect.

One of Griffin's misdeeds does provide a cynical view of human nature. When he robs a bank, he throws the money in the street. Everybody goes after the loot but no one returns it. It's a Depression-era commentary on the public's desperation and their mistrust of banks. It's hard to imagine a depiction of self-serving, unethical behavior in a post-Code film. It's not just because the enforced Code would have forbidden scenes of people stealing without being punished. By the mid-1930s, Americans' faith in the country's economic survival was renewed due to the Roosevelt Administration's ambitious New Deal programs. Of course, *The Invisible Man*, like the book, takes place in England, but by the time the Code was strengthened, Americans wouldn't have identified with the money grabbers as strongly as they did in 1933.

The same Americans probably identified with the invisible man to a certain extent. Jack Griffin is, in his words, "a poor, struggling chemist," and he hopes that his invisibility formula will make him wealthy. It doesn't, but it does give him potential "power to rule, to make the world grovel at my feet." He uses his unseen state to go after people he considers a thorn in his side, particularly the inquisitive landlady Jenny Hall (Una O'Connor), and he relishes humiliating the authorities. Griffin may be a psychopath, but his joy in creating chaos is infectious, thanks to Claude Rains' enthusiastic voice work. Even though Rains isn't seen until the end, *The Invisible Man* was as much a star-making vehicle for him as *Frankenstein* was for Boris Karloff.

As long as the invisible man engages in harmless havoc like stealing a constable's trousers, one can't help but laugh with him. Griffin ultimately pays for his crimes, but he has a heck of a great time when he's committing them. At least some frustrated Americans must have envied him; if *they* could become unseen, at least they could temporarily experience freedom and power. Of all the pre-Code horror fiends, Jack Griffin is the most oddly alluring. Had *The Invisible Man* been released later in the 1930s or in the following decade, Griffin would not have seemed attractive to filmgoers. This had nothing to do with the Production Code. Paul Jensen points out, "This fascination [with an omnipotent figure] faded . . . as the Depression receded and reports from Germany revealed some of the realistic results of putting the Superman philosophy into practice."

Unlike the titular character in H.G. Wells' novel, Griffin repents of his actions in the end. His last words are, "I meddled in things that man should leave alone." R.C. Sherriff and James Whale must have given the cinematic Griffin an epiphany in order to ensure audience identification and sympathy. In the book, Griffin is a callous misanthrope even before he becomes unseen, whereas in the film, he is a decent, well-meaning man who becomes criminally insane due to a fictitious drug, monocaine. But Sherriff and Whale also satisfied the Production Code when they gave the invisible man a last-minute moral awakening. Even before the Code was strengthened, it still had some influence in dictating morality in the movies.

Another concession to the Code was reassuring film audiences that once Griffin died, the world wouldn't have to worry about another invisible menace. In the novel, the transparent criminal recruits a drunken tramp named Thomas Marvel to be a visible accomplice. But the hobo pilfers Griffin's scientific books. The book's epilogue establishes that Marvel has profited from telling theatergoers about his experiences with the invisible man. He uses the money to establish an inn, and when he's alone there, he examines the books to decipher Griffin's formula. Wells ends the story with the open-ended passage: "And none other will know of them until he dies."

Why was Thomas Marvel dropped from the film adaptation? Obviously, Universal wanted to make the invisible man more menacing than he was in the book. The studio was determined to make him an awe-inspiring behemoth like RKO's *King Kong*. The cinematic invisible man kills a lot more people and commits greater crimes than his literary counterpart. An unseen malefactor who is hoodwinked by a vagabond would not impress thrill-seeking filmgoers.

Universal also provided the film with an unambiguous conclusion because the studio didn't want to suggest that a sequel was in the works. Ironically, in 1940, a sequel *was* filmed, *The Invisible Man Returns*. In this movie, Griffin's younger brother Frank (John Sutton) uses the formula on a wrongly-condemned man, Geoffrey Radcliffe (Vincent Price), in order to nab the real culprit. Unlike Jack Griffin, Radcliffe becomes visible and remains alive by the film's end. The Code was in full force by 1940; Price's character couldn't take lives if he was expected to survive when the credits rolled. Geoffrey merely teases and threatens the lawmen and the people who framed him. A bunch of *Invisible* spinoffs followed, culminating in 1951's *Abbott and Costello Meet the Invisible Man*. Only in *The Invisible Man's Revenge* (1944) did Universal's transparent protagonist revert to criminality. (Incidentally, this invisible character was a Robert Griffin, no relation to Jack, played by Jon Hall.)

The Invisible Man was an enormous box office success that single-handedly saved the financially-ailing Universal. When the film premiered at the Roxy in New York City, it broke box office records, attracting eighty thousand patrons in four days. But that didn't mean that everyone who saw the film approved of it. "Please do not let us see any more such horrible, gruesome productions," wrote Mrs. Lloyd C. Gilchrist of Springfield, Vermont to the journal *Silver Screen*. "In our way of thinking its [sic] entirely out of the question for the youth of today to see such a picture." Adults in a survey conducted by the Parents-Teachers Association of Pelham, New York agreed with Mrs. Gilchrist; *The Invisible Man* was unsuitable for teenagers and children. Yet in the same survey, male grade school and high school students rated the film among the "best pictures they had ever seen," highlighting a generation gap.

The naysayers had no impact on *The Invisible Man*; the critics loved the film as much as the public. They may have enjoyed it not only because it was well made and because Rains was excellent but because unlike other pre-Code horrors, its shocks were restrained. Silver Screen assured its readers despite Mrs. Gilchrist's complaints, "You won't go home and have nightmares after this [viewing] the way you did after *Frankenstein* and *Dracula*...." *Motion Picture Herald*'s critic wrote, "... *The Invisible Man* is dramatic rather than gruesome and situations and reactions precipitate easing comedy contrasts."

Even the book's author H.G. Wells, who hated *The Island of Lost Souls,* enjoyed Universal's treatment of *The Invisible Man*. He did object to the film's concept of the invisibility formula as a mind-altering drug: "If the man had remained sane, we should have had the inherent monstrosity of an ordinary man in this extraordinary position. But instead of an Invisible Man, we now have an Invisible Lunatic!" James Whale, as witty a person as he was a director, pointed out, "If a man said to you that he was about to make himself invisible, wouldn't you think he was crazy already?"

Actually, Whale and R.C. Sherriff originally intended Griffin to go mad because of his inability to reverse the formula's effects. They decided that this conflict could not be effectively dramatized on film, so they devised the drug "monocaine" to explain Jack's monstrous behavior. Had Whale and Sherriff been faithful to Wells' concept of Griffin as a sociopath from the start, filmgoers wouldn't have sympathized with Griffin. They probably wouldn't have been as enthusiastic about the film. The cinematic invisible man may have been a horrific character, but people could identify with him to a certain extent. And unlike his literary counterpart, he was a truly tragic figure.

The Invisible Man was an exception among pre-Code horrors; it not only avoided major controversy, but it enjoyed critical respectability. This would not be the case for Universal's next horror film, the first teaming of Boris Karloff and Bela Lugosi. Although ostensibly based on an Edgar Allan Poe work, the resulting movie, *The Black Cat,* would be even less faithful to the original than *Murders in the Rue Morgue.* Years later, Karloff wryly commented, "Poor Poe. The things we did to him when he wasn't there to defend himself!" By then a wealthy and beloved star, Boris could look back and laugh about it. But back in 1934, the production of *The Black Cat* was no laughing matter, especially to the Production Code Administration and the Legion of Decency.

THE BLACK CAT (1934)

Released May 3, 1934; A Universal Picture; *Director:* **Edgar G. Ulmer;** *Producer:* **Carl Laemmle, Jr.;** *Screenplay:* **Peter Ruric, from a story by Edgar G. Ulmer and Peter Ruric, suggested by Edgar Allan Poe's tale;** *Supervisor:* **E.M. Asher;** *Art Director:* **Charles D. Hall;** *Musical Director:* **Heinz Roemheld;** *Film Editor:* **Ray Curtiss;** *Special Effects:* **John P. Fulton;** *Makeup Artist:* **Jack P. Pierce; 65 minutes.**

Cast: **Boris Karloff (Hjalmar Poelzig), Bela Lugosi (Dr. Vitus Werdegast), David Manners (Peter Alison), Jacqueline Wells [aka Julie Bishop] (Joan Alison), Lucille Lund (Karen), Egon Brecher (The Majordomo), Harry Cording (Thamal), Henry Armetta (The Sergeant), Albert Conti (The Lieutenant), Anna Duncan (The Maid) Andre Cheron (Train Conductor), George Davis (Bus Driver), Alphonse Martell (A Porter), Tony Marlow (A Patrolman), Paul Weigel (Stationmaster).**

SYNOPSIS: American honeymooners Peter and Joan Alison meet Hungarian psychiatrist Dr. Vitus Werdegast on a train bound for a resort town in Hungary. Werdegast has just been released from a nightmarish prison camp after fifteen years. After the three disembark at the town, they take a bus during a storm, but the vehicle crashes and the driver is killed. The Alisons and Werdegast seek refuge in the lair of Austrian architect Hjalmar Poelzig. Poelzig has constructed this house on the ruins of Fort Marmaros, which he once commanded during World War I. Poelzig and Werdegast had fought in the Austro-Hungarian army during the conflict but Poelzig sold the Fort to the Russians, resulting in the deaths of Hungarians and Werdegast's imprisonment. Poelzig also took Werdegast's wife and daughter away from him and Werdegast wants them back. The necrophil-

iac Poelzig killed Werdegast's wife. Her embalmed corpse is in a glass case, and Poelzig shows it to the aghast Werdegst. Poelzig is now married to Werdegast's daughter Karen, who doesn't realize her father is still alive. Poelzig kills Karen so she won't see her father again. He holds the Alisons hostage and plans to sacrifice Joan in a Satanic ceremony. Werdegast rescues Joan, but when he sees Karen's corpse, he goes completely mad. The vengeful Werdegast ties Poelzig to a rack and skins him alive. He tells the Alisons to leave the house, and then he pulls a lever that sets off explosions that demolish Poelzig's lair. The Alisons flee to safety on a train to Budapest.

If Hollywood's first pre-Code horror, *Dracula*, handled the shocks with restraint and trepidation, then Hollywood's final pre-Code horror, *The Black Cat*, tackles the shocks with boldness and relish. This film is a lurid catalog of depravity—necrophilia, Satan worship, virgin sacrifice, and torture. The central conflict is between a degenerate who scorns all of society's morals and proprieties and a maniac hell-bent on homicidal revenge. The public loved it, making it a box office hit. Indeed, it made more money than any of Universal's other 1934 releases. But *The Black Cat* aroused the ire of censors and moralists. Less than two months after its release, the studios, fearful of government censorship, would fully enforce the Production Code.

Incredibly, the original cut of *The Black Cat* was even more outrageous. In the initial version, Werdegast loses his sanity after seeing his wife's corpse and tries to rape Joan. But the Universal brass, revolted when viewing the newly-completed film, judged it *too* outrageous for the film-going public. Ulmer assembled the cast and crew for a rushed three-and-a-half days of retakes. Gruesome dramatizations, particularly Poelzig's flaying, were toned down. Werdegast's character was softened, no longer lusting after Joan. Lugosi, weary of being typecast as a fiend, was delighted by the character revisions.

Yet during the retakes, Ulmer successfully defied the censors by adding a new scene. It consisted of Poelzig strolling through the cellars, scrutinizing his embalmed victims. In the released film, these unfortunate women, sacrificed in satanic rites, are embalmed in vertical glass coffins. Why did the Universal brass permit this scene? The wily Ulmer sensed that they weren't sophisticated enough to recognize the scene's perverse implications.

Lucille Lund played one of the corpses, Karen's mother. Posing in the glass coffin was an excruciating experience: "[The crew] had a big hook at the top and they twisted my very long hair ... around that hook, so it looked like it was standing straight up. Then they had a little contraption—sort of like a pair of canvas panties that they put me in, that went up under my long robes; these were suspended by wires so I was lifted, and my feet were dangling, and it appeared I was hanging from my hair. I was virtually hanging in that little 'panty,' and there was no way I could get out of that glass coffin unless somebody lifted me out and took me out." One day, when Ulmer told everybody to take a lunch break, he left Lucille hanging there for an hour out of spite; she had spurned his sexual advances. The director was almost as cruel as the fictional Poelzig. Karloff, though, was very nice toward Lucille; she called him "the most delightful, charming man you could ever meet—just altogether lovely."

The character of Hjalmar Poelzig was inspired by an actual person who lived up to his soubriquet "The Wickedest Man in the World." He was Aleister Crowley, a British occultist whose credo was "Do what thou wilt / shall be the whole of the Law." He established a temple in a farmhouse in Cefalu, Sicily called the Abbey of Thelema. There, he indulged in all kinds of debaucheries, particularly bizarre rites celebrating bestiality. Eventually, Crowley's depraved antics got him in trouble with the law. On February 16, 1923, Raoul Loveday, an Oxford undergraduate, died at the Abbey. It was rumored, but never verified, that his death resulted from drinking a sacrificial cat's blood. Nevertheless, Benito Mussolini deported Crowley. The fascist despot would later prevent *The Black Cat* from being shown in Italy with the explanation, "Because it may create horror."

In 1932, artist Nina Hamnett wrote a shocking account of the occultist in her memoir. Claiming to know Crowley, she contended that he practiced black magic at the Abbey of Thelema and may had been responsible for a baby's mysterious disappearance. The villagers of Cefaulu "were frightened of him," she wrote. Crowley sued her for defamation in the same year *The Black Cat* was released. Not only did he lose in court, but the judge insisted that he pay the defendant's legal costs. Already financially strapped, Crowley declared bankruptcy. This was fortunate for Universal since he couldn't sue the studio. Soon the world lost interest in "The Wickedest Man in the World," and he died a forgotten figure on December 1, 1947.

When *The Black Cat* played at cinemas during the Depression, Crowley was still big news. Perhaps so many people flocked to the film out of morbid curiosity—did the film accurately depict Crowley's twisted behavior? Did the filmmakers, like Nina Hamnett, have the inside dirt about the Wickedest Man in the World? What is obvious is that moviegoers were primarily interested in Karloff's Crowley-like villain as well as Lugosi's tormented antagonist. They didn't care about the innocent couple played by David Manners and Jacqueline Wells. The following year, Universal didn't reteam *them* in another Poe-inspired shocker, *The Raven*—they reteamed Karloff and Lugosi. The studio was not daunted by the newly-strengthened Production Code.

The public didn't pay any attention to the critics, a few of whom actually liked the film, albeit with reservations. For instance, the San Francisco *Examiner* considered *The Black Cat* to be "the most cultured horror film ... yet witnessed" and "a film to be watched with considerable pleasure." But the reviewer believed, "It never, for all its careful staging manages to catch the mood of horror its story calls for." Most reviewers panned the film. Some of them found *The Black Cat*'s shocks unconvincing. *The New York Times* found the film "more foolish than horrible," and *Time* called it "a dismal hocus-pocus which ... fails to frighten the audience...." *Time* particularly found the Satan worship scene ridiculous: "Silly shot: the Black Mass, with Karloff intoning Latin gibberish."

Even some of *The Black Cat*'s suggestive elements are idiosyncratic. When Poelzig first meets Joan, she is in a daze. Since she has been injured in the crash, Werdegast has put her under sedation, and she has just revived. Seemingly bewitched, Joan passionately kisses Peter. While she does this, cameraman John J. Mescall focuses on Poelzig's frenzied reaction—he grasps a nude female statue on his desk, symbolizing his desire to use Joan for his own perverse aims. Later, when Hjalmar is at the chess table, he fondles the breasts of one of the game pieces, a queen. Once again the filmmakers signify his nefarious intentions.

The climactic flaying scene, as filmed under Ulmer's direction, is a bizarre mixture of brazenness and restraint. The Satan-worshiping Poelzig is tied to a rack like a crucified Christ, recalling the earlier image of Arlene Francis's bound prostitute in *Murders in the Rue Morgue*. Werdegast bluntly tells his intended victim, "Did you ever see an animal *skinned*, Hjalmar? Ha, ha! That's what I am going to do to you now. Tear the skin from your body—slowly—bit by bit!" Vitus carries out his threat, but the audience doesn't see the graphic results. Instead, Ulmer shows the skinning segment in silhouette, as the Production Code insisted. Still, the scene's grisliness comes across thanks to Poelzig's pained scream and Joan's horrified reaction.

Would this scene be allowed in a post-Code film? It may have been toned down a bit, but it likely would have been accepted by the censors. The atrocity is shown in shadows. In 1944's *House of Frankenstein*, Dracula in bat form feeds on a victim's throat. This horrific act is also shown in shadows. Even Poelzig's Christ-like posture would probably be approved; Karloff is bound in the same way in 1935's *The Bride of Frankenstein*.

Despite his character's gruesome comeuppance, Karloff relished the role. In an interview with *Screen Play* magazine, he explained the appeal of playing villains like Poelzig: "It dates right back to Mother Eve, who perhaps revealed that Evil is much more fascinating than Good when she allowed the serpent to merchandize his apple. There's a little bit of evil in us all ... Most people- even most actors—don't get the chance that is mine to indulge this inherently bad streak...."

Boris was being facetious, but he touched on an essential fact: fiends like Poelzig were perversely appealing. He may pay for his sins, but like previous evildoers (Leslie Banks' Count Zaroff and Lionel Atwill's Eric Gorman come to mind), he has the time of his life when committing them. As Danny Reid points out in his review of *The Black Cat* on his website Pre-Code.com, "... Satanism never really gets to look like this much fun again for a few decades."

If Karloff's Poelzig was an alluring villain to filmgoers, then Lugosi's Werdegast was a sympathetic madman. Like Lionel Atwill's Ivan Igor in *Mystery of the Wax Museum*, Vitus's insanity was caused by his suffering, inflicted on him by another person for his own gain. In this case, Poelzig was the malefactor. Fascinated as audiences were with Hjalmar, they were also appalled by him. Werdegast's retribution, extreme as it was, fulfilled the viewers' bitter wishes for Poelzig's punishment. Despite his psychosis, Vitus is *The Black Cat*'s hero. It is he, not the romantic lead Peter Alison, who saves Joan from being sacrificed. And Vitus nobly spares the newlyweds' lives when he demolishes Hjalmar's fortress, which includes himself and his "rotten cult" (Werdegast's description).

The Black Cat does not mention anything about the Depression. The film, however, comments on the lingering after effects of World War I in Continental Europe. The two central characters, Hjalmar Poelzig, and Vitus Werdegast, are veterans of the Austro-Hungarian Army. Poelzig betrayed Werdegast and the other soldiers by secretly dealing with the enemy Russia. Vitus tells Hjalmar, "Those who died were fortunate. I was taken prisoner—to Kurgaal. Kurgaal, where the soul is killed—slowly." Kurgaal is a fictitious Russian POW camp devised for the film, but Vitus's situation does touch on the real traumas of World War I POWs. Lugosi had actually served in the Austro-Hungarian Army and was wounded on the Russian front.

The United States remained uninvolved in the international conflict until 1917, nearly three years after it started. Siding with the Allies, America contributed to their victory over the Central Powers (including Austria-Hungary) in 1918, but the actual warfare was on the European continent. By the time *The Black Cat* was released, the United States was at peace and not involved in international affairs. Peter and Joan Alison represent innocent Americans who stumble upon the ravages of World War I in Europe. (Ironically, David Manners, who played Peter, was born in Canada.)

By focusing on the war in Europe, *The Black Cat* could not offend American sensibilities. But the Austrian government, a right-wing dictatorship, protested "that one main figure, an Austrian, is shown as [a] military traitor and main criminal, thus offending the national feeling of the people." Finding Poelzig's character as objectionable as the film's depiction of devil worship, the government prevented *The Black Cat* from being shown in Austria.

Surprisingly, church groups did not find *The Black Cat* blasphemous. In the spring of 1934, the Detroit Council of Catholic Organizations graded current film releases for the publication *Michigan Catholic*. These films were divided into three categories: Classes A, B, and C. Class A was given to films the organization considered acceptable for all ages. Class B films "[m]ay be considered offensive, because they are suggestive in spots, vulgar, sophisticated, or lacking in modesty." Class C films were condemned as "[i]mmoral and indecent . . . it may be said that they are unsuitable for any decent person." These ratings were endorsed by Catholic and Protestant organizations in the United States. *The Black Cat* was given a "B" rating. So subtle were the film's horror and sexual overtones that they likely went over the Detroit Council's heads, just as they likely went over the critics' heads. Perhaps if every film released at this time was as subtle as *The Black Cat*, the newly-formed Catholic Legion of Decency wouldn't have successfully coerced Hollywood to invigorate the Production Code. But of course, the Code was strengthened. Although this did not eliminate horror films, it would profoundly affect them for many years.

AFTERWORD

How did the strengthened Production Code affect the horror genre? Initially, fright films seemed to survive stricter censorship guidelines. The year 1935 was especially prolific. Universal reunited James Whale, Boris Karloff, and Colin Clive for a sequel to *Frankenstein* called *The Bride of Frankenstein*, reteamed Karloff and Bela Lugosi in another chiller loosely inspired by Edgar Allan Poe called *The Raven*, and produced its first werewolf film, *Werewolf of London*. MGM reunited Tod Browning and Bela Lugosi for *The Mark of the Vampire* and introduced American filmgoers to Hungarian actor Peter Lorre in the mad scientist shocker *Mad Love*. Columbia released its first full-fledged horror film *The Black Room* with Boris Karloff playing good and evil twins. Even two minor studios provided moviegoers with horror films: Republic with *The Crime of Dr. Crespi* and Invincible Pictures Corporation with *Condemned to Live*.

Most of these films did good business at the box office, indicating that American filmgoers still enjoyed being frightened. *The Bride of Frankenstein* was especially successful, boosting Boris Karloff's reputation as the King of Horror. Only *Mad Love* lost money, possibly because the public considered it too gruesome to be entertaining. (In this film, Colin Clive is a pianist who loses his hands in a train accident; demented surgeon Peter Lorre provides him with the severed hands of an executed murderer.) A Long Island exhibitor complained, "The producers must have been mad to even attempt such a piece as this. This is certainly a black eye for M-G-M ... *Mad Love* is the type of picture that brought about censorship."

The PCA was leery about horror films, even though most of them were profitable. The PCA wanted to *discourage* the studios from making horror films. The British Board of Censors in the United Kingdom also continued to fret about Hollywood's fright films. In the past, it had banned *Freaks* and *The Island of Lost Souls*. On August 23, 1935, an Associated Press story in the United States claimed that the British Board vowed not to allow any more horror films in the United Kingdom. In fact, the Board continued to permit subsequent American shockers to be shown there and even produced one the following year starring native Britisher Boris Karloff, *The Man Who Changed His Mind*. (In 1937, however, the Board did give all horror films an "H" certificate. The "H" stood for "Horrific," suggesting that only adults should see them.)

The PCA overreacted to the Associated Press account. Whether the PCA genuinely worried about Hollywood's box office prospects in Britain or whether it took advantage of the story to pursue their anti-horror agenda, the organization repeatedly warned the studios that it was foolhardy to continue creating scary products. The PCA saw to it that the macabre content of three 1936 films were considerably softened—Warner Brothers' *The Walking Dead*, Universal's *Dracula's Daughter*, and MGM's *The Devil Doll*. Bela Lugosi was one casualty of the PCA's meddling. Universal wanted him to reprise his vampire role for *Dracula's Daughter* but then dropped him from the sequel. According to *The Hollywood Reporter*, the studio decided that the vampire "will stay dead" because "recent condemnations of undue horror stuff decided the studio to let him lay."

At the end of the 1935-36 season, the studios caved in and temporarily abandoned horror films. This especially affected Lugosi; the typecast bogeyman appeared in only one film in 1937, the serial *S.O.S. Coast Guard*, and appeared in no films in 1938. Boris Karloff remained active, but Hollywood didn't consider him marketable in non-horror films. Although he had a contract with Warner Brothers, he took a pay cut after appearing in three films.

Although Hollywood avoided making new horror films, it could not prevent cinemas from reviving earlier ones. In August 1938, E. Mark Umann, manager of Los Angeles' Regina Theatre, screened *Dracula* and *Frankenstein* for four days. So many people flocked to see them that Umann had to turn some patrons away. Universal got the message: it hired Karloff and Lugosi for a new sequel, *Son of Frankenstein*. The PCA attempted unsuccessfully to dissuade the studio from making the film. Upon its release, *Son of Frankenstein* was a box office smash. Horror films were back in vogue.

Universal and other studios created many fright films between 1939 and 1946. As the years progressed, Universal's chillers became less artistic and more juvenile. This wasn't due to any concerns about offending patrons but because the studio became more concerned about profits than quality. At RKO, Val Lewton produced intelligent shockers like *Cat People*, where the horrors were suggested rather than shown. Not surprisingly, these restrained shockers thrived under the vigorous Production Code. Lewton, however, refrained from overt scares not because he wanted to please the PCA but for aesthetic purposes. The other studios' fright flicks, like those in the pre-Code period, varied in quality from artfully-made shockers (Twentieth Century Fox's *The Lodger* and MGM's *The Picture of Dorian Gray*, for example) to sloppily-made potboilers (just about all of low-budget Monogram's product, for instance).

By the end of 1946, Hollywood stopped making horror films. This had nothing to do with the Production Code. World War II had ended with the atomic bombings of Hiroshima and Nagasaki. Horror scholar Gregory William Mank points out, "In the true horrors of atomic mutants, flag-shrouded coffins, the boy-next-door home from the war without arms or legs or face, the midnight shows of a Monster stitched together from the dead or a vampire lusting after maiden's blood seemed neither appetizing, nor frightening."

The premier horror studio Universal was running dry on inspiration, grinding out sequels and dreary mysteries masquerading as shockers. On October 1, 1946, Universal merged with International Pictures to become Universal-International. This new organization pledged to release only "A" pictures. Since Universal's horrors had long ago been regulated to "B" status, they were immediately discarded. Universal-International even sold a completed shocker, *The Brute Man*, to the low-budget studio Producers Releasing Corporation. Meanwhile, Val Lewton left RKO for non-horror work at Paramount after making his last shocker, *Bedlam* (1946). The other studios followed Universal-International and RKO in abandoning fright flicks.

Universal-International briefly revived the Frankenstein Monster, Dracula, and the Wolf Man (who first appeared as the title character in the 1941 hit) to menace the studio's popular comedy team in *Abbott and Costello Meet Frankenstein*. The film's commercial success persuaded the studio to pit the duo against other classic monsters like the Invisible Man before putting the fiends completely out to pasture. Horror made a comeback in the 1950s, but most of these new chillers were science fiction films playing on Americans' fears of the Red Menace and atomic destruction.

Around the same time, the Production Code began to weaken due to a combination of factors. With the rise of television, the American film industry worried about how to attract people to cinemas. In 1952, the Supreme Court ruled that movies, like other mediums, were constitutionally entitled to freedom of expression. Audacious filmmakers like Otto Preminger and Billy Wilder, agreeing with the ruling, began challenging the Code. "Foreign" films, which were not subject to the Code, also competed with domestic films on the market.

Among the "foreign" films that appealed to American filmgoers were new horror films produced by British studio Hammer. In the late 1950s, the studio made new versions of the classic horror films *Frankenstein, Dracula,* and *The Mummy.* Unlike the originals, these films were not only in glorious color but dealt more frankly with sex and violence. As the 1950s ended, American film companies handled horror films more boldly. The British-born director Alfred Hitchcock was a notable influence with his 1960 chiller *Psycho.* Tame by today's standards, it was incredibly grim and brutal viewing for American filmgoers when it was initially released. More importantly for the film industry, it was an enormous box office success.

In 1963, filmmaker Herschell Gordon Lewis devised a new subgenre that would have been unthinkable even in the pre-Code era: the splatter film. As the title *Blood Feast* suggested, it was exceedingly gory. Critics reviled the film, calling it tasteless and amateurish, but the public couldn't get enough of it, so Lewis ground out more of them throughout the rest of the decade. The 1960s was also a time when American society openly challenged traditional values, particularly sexual mores. The shrewd filmmakers produced bolder films that reflected these attitudes. Finally in 1968, the Production Code collapsed. It was replaced by the Motion Picture Association of America film rating system, which determined whether or not the films are suitable for family viewing. Of course, this rating system still exists today.

Television may have been a bane to the film industry in the 1950s, but it introduced younger people to the pre-Code shockers. People who hadn't been born when these films were originally made marveled at what they saw, even if some of them, like *Frankenstein*, were edited. *Famous Monsters of Filmland* and other fright film magazines proliferated in the 1960s to celebrate these groundbreaking works that initiated the horror genre. That same decade signified the reemergence of Rouben Mamoulian's *Dr. Jekyll and Mr. Hyde* and the rediscovery of *The Old Dark House*. In 1970, a print of *Mystery of the Wax Museum*, long believed lost, was found in a private vault, and it was soon shown in revival theaters and on television.

Today, all the pre-Code horrors (with the exception of *The Monkey's Paw*) are commercially available on home video and are still screened in revival theaters. They are discussed on the Internet, particularly online forums like the Classic Horror Film Board and Scarlet Street. Seeing these films, it's easy to understand why they are still remembered over eighty years after they first premiered in cinemas. The best ones, like *Frankenstein*, *The Mummy*, and *King Kong*, transcend their Depression-era origins and like all classics have enduring appeal. But even the more dated ones like *The Mask of Fu Manchu* are fascinating time capsules, providing insight on how filmmakers experimented with horror in the pre-Code era. It was a time that was permissive in some ways and restrictive in other ways. The films were not always successful, but they were always interesting. Today's moviemakers could never duplicate them because the period in which these horrors were made is now history.

BIBLIOGRAPHY

BOOKS

Connell. Richard. "Most Dangerous Game." In *The Ghouls*. Ed. by Peter Haining. New York, NY: Stein and Day, 1971. 154-69.

Curtis, James. *James Whale: A New World of Gods and Monsters*. Boston, MA: Faber & Faber, 1998.

Doherty, Thomas Patrick. *Pre-code Hollywood: Sex, Immorality, and Insurrection in American Cinema; 1930-1934*. New York, NY: Columbia University Press, 1999.

Everson, William K. *Classics of the Horror Film*. Secaucus, NJ: Citadel Press, 1974.

Goldner, Orville and George E. Turner. *The Making of King Kong: The Story Behind a Film Classic*. South Brunswick, NJ: A.S. Barnes, 1975.

Hogan, David J. *Dark Romance: Sexuality in the Horror Film*. Jefferson, NC: McFarland & Company, Inc., 1986.

Humphries, Reynold. *The Hollywood Horror Film 1931-1941: Madness in a Social Landscape*. Lanham, MD: The Scarecrow Press, 2006.

Jensen, Paul. *The Men Who Made the Monsters*. New York, NY: Twayne Publishers, 1996.

Johnson, Tom. *Censored Screams: The British Ban on Hollywood Horror in the Thirties*. Jefferson, NC: McFarland & Company, Inc., 1997.

Kinnard, Roy and Tony Crnkovich. *The Films of Fay Wray*. Jefferson, NC: McFarland & Company, 2005.

Koszarski, Richard, ed. *Mystery of the Wax Museum*. Madison, WI: The University of Wisconsin Press, 1979.

Leider, Emily W. *Myrna Loy: The Only Good Girl in Hollywood*. Berkeley, CA: University of California Press, 2011.

Lennig, Arthur. *The Immortal Count: The Life and Films of Bela Lugosi*. Lexington, KY: University of Kentucky Press, 2010.

Lindsay, Cynthia. *Dear Boris: The Life of William Henry Pratt a.k.a. Boris Karloff.* New York, NY: Alfred A. Knopf, 1975.

Mank, Gregory William. *Bela Lugosi and Boris Karloff: The Expanded Story of a Haunting Collaboration, with a Complete Filmography of Their Films Together.* Jefferson, NC: McFarland & Company, Inc., 2009.

_____. *Hollywood Cauldron: Thirteen Horror Films From the Genre's Golden Age.* Jefferson, NC : McFarland & Company, 1994.

_____. *The Very Witching Time of Night: Dark Alleys of Classic Horror Cinema.* Jefferson, NC: McFarland & Company, 2014.

_____. *Women in Horror Films, 1930s.* Jefferson, NC: McFarland & Company, 1999.

Nollen, Scott Allen. *Boris Karloff: A Critical Account of His Screen, Stage, Radio, Television and Recording Work.* Jefferson, NC: McFarland & Company, 2008.

Poe, Edgar Allan. "Murders in the Rue Morgue." In *Edgar Allan Poe: The Fall of the House of Usher and Other Tales.* New York, NY: Signet Classics, 2006. 44-79.

Priestley, J.B. *Benighted.* Kansas City, MO: Valancourt Books, 2013.

Rhodes, Gary D., ed. *Edgar G. Ulmer: Detour on Poverty Row.* Lanham, MD: Lexington Books, 2008.

Rhodes, Gary D. *White Zombie: Anatomy of a Horror Film.* Jefferson, NC: McFarland & Company, 2001.

Robbins, Tod. "Freaks." In *The Ghouls.* Ed. by Peter Haining. New York, NY: Stein and Day, 1971. 137-53.

Senn, Bryan. *Golden Horrors: An Illustrated Critical Filmography, 1931-1939.* Jefferson, NC: McFarland & Company, Inc., 1996.

Shelley, Mary. *Frankenstein.* London, U.K.: Everyman, 2004.

Skal, David J. *The Monster Show: A Cultural History of Horror.* New York, NY: W.W. Norton & Company, 1993.

Stevenson, Robert Louis. "The Strange Case of Dr. Jekyll and Mr. Hyde." In *The Strange Case of Dr. Jekyll and Mr. Hyde The Merry Men and Other Tales and Fables.* Hertfordshire, U.K.: Wordsworth Classics, 1999. 3-54.

Stoker, Bram. *Dracula.* New York, NY: Signet Classic, 1992.

Vaz, Mark Cotta. *Living Dangerously: The Adventures of Merian C. Cooper, Creator of King Kong.* New York, NY: Villard, 2005.

Vieira, Mark A. *Hollywood Horror: From Gothic to Cosmic.* New York, NY: Harry N. Abrams, Inc., 2003.

_____. *Irving Thalberg: Boy Wonder to Producer Prince.* Berkeley, CA: University of California Press, 2010.

_____. *Sin in Soft Focus: Pre-Code Hollywood.* New York, NY: Harry N. Abrams, Inc., 1999.

Weaver, Tom and Michael and John Brunas. *Universal Horrors: The Studio's Classic Films, 1931-1946. Second Edition.* Jefferson, NC: McFarland & Company, 2007.

Wells, H.G. *The Invisible Man: A Grotesque Romance.* Rockville, MD: Phoenix Pick, 2008.

_____. *The Island of Dr. Moreau.* New York, NY: The Modern Library, 2002.

ARTICLES

MacQueen, Scott. "Doctor X- A Technicolor Landmark." *American Cinematographer* 67 (June 1986): 34-42.

_____. "The Mystery of the Wax Museum." *American Cinematographer* 71 (April 1990): 42-50.

Price, Michael H. and George Turner. "Behind 'The Mask of Fu Manchu.'" *American Cinematographer* 76 (January 1995): 68-74.

Turner, George. "Hunting 'The Most Dangerous Game.'" *American Cinematographer* 68 (September 1987): 40-8.

WEBSITES

Greenbriar Picture Shows:
http://greenbriarpictureshows.blogspot.com/

Hollywoodland A Site About Hollywood and Its History:
http://allanellenberger.com/

The Irish Journal of Gothic and Horror Studies:
http://irishgothichorrorjournal.homestead.com

Lantern: Search, Visualize & Explore the Media History Digital Library: http://lantern.mediahist.org/

Olga Baclanova: The Ultimate Cinemantrap: http://www.olgabaclanova.com/

Only the Cinema: http://seul-le-cinema.blogspot.com/

Pre-Code.com: http://pre-code.com/

Abbott and Costello Meet Frankenstein (1948), 159

INDEX

Abbott and Costello Meet Frankenstein (1948), 159
Abbott and Costello Meet the Invisible Man (1951), 145
Academy for the Motion Pictures Arts and Sciences, 29
Ackerman, Forrest J., 106
Acquanetta, 104
Adams, Stella, 108
Ager, Cecilia, 105
Alexandra, Czarina of the Russias, 89
American Society for the Prevention of Cruelty to Animals (ASPCA), 130
Ames, Leon, 33
Anderson, Esther, 60
Ape, The (1940), 92
Arlen, Richard, 100
Armstrong, Robert, 67, 124
Athenaeum, The (periodical), 100
Atwill, Lionel, vi, viii, 53, 57, 61, 64, 94, 106, 109, 110-11, 114, 115, 116, 118, 125, 126, 128, 129, 130, 132, 133, 137, 153, 154

Baclanova, Olga, 41
Balderston, John L., 94
Banks, Leslie, 64, 66, 68, 153
Barnell, Jane, 42, 46
Barrymore, Ethel, 89
Barrymore, John, 2, 18, 25
Barrymore, Lionel, 89
Bedlam (1946), 159
Bellamy, Madge, 49, 50, 102
Belmore, Lionel, 108
Ben Ali (Lexington, KY), 60
Benighted (novel), 72, 73, 74, 76
Bennett, Leila, 57

Bettendorf, Henry, 76
Betty Boop (cartoon character), v, 124
Bishop, Julie (see Wells, Jacqueline), 152
Black Cat, The (1934) (film), viii, 37, 115, 146, **149-55**
"Black Cat, The" (short story), 146
Black Room, The (1935), 157
Blaidsell, George, 69
Blood Feast (1963), 160
Boleslawski, Richard, 89
Bond, Lillian, 74, 75
Brabin, Charles, 89
Breen, Joseph, 132
Brenner, W.H., 131
Bride of Frankenstein, The (1935), 24, 153, 157
British Board of Censors, The, 157, 158
Browning, Tod, 2, 3, 5, 6, 7, 8, 40, 41, 43, 44, 45, 46, 157
Brownlow, Kevin, 123
Brunas, John, 8, 34, 72
Brunas, Michael, 8, 34, 72
Brute Man, The (1946), 159
Burke, Kathleen, 100, 101, 102, 105, 129, 131
Byron, Arthur, 94

Cameron, Kate, 104
Canova, Antonio, 24
Capitol Theatre (Atlanta, GA), 3-4
Capitol Theatre (London, UK), 77
Capitol Theatre (New York, NY), 90
Captive Wild Woman (1943), 104
Carewe, Arthur Edmund, 58, 114
Carolina Theatre (Greenville, SC), 60
Carradine, John, 104
Cat and the Canary, The (1927), 73

Cat People (1942), 159
Censored Screams: The British Ban on Hollywood Horror in the Thirties (book), 23, 49, 96
Chandler, Helen, 5, 6
Chaney, Lon, 2, 3, 6, 7
Chaney, Lon, Jr., 109
Chatterton, Ruth, 25
Citizen Kane (1941), 86
Clarke, Betsy Ross, 37
Clarke, Mae, 14, 18, 72
Classic Horror Film Board (online forum), 161
Classics of the Horror Film (book), 77, 128, 131
Clive, Colin, 15, 16, 157
Colbert, Claudette, 25
Collier's (periodical), 64
Columbia Pictures, 157
Condemned to Live (1935), 157
Connell, Richard, 64, 66
Conway, Jack, 40
Cooper, Jackie, 28
Cooper, Merian C., 64, 65, 112, 123
Corrigan, D'Arcy, 34
Cosmopolitan Productions, 86
Court Street Theatre (Buffalo, NY), 44
Cozy Theatre (Winchester, IN), 131
Creelman, James, 64, 68
Crime of Dr. Crespi, The (1935), 157
Crowley, Aleister, 151, 152
Curtis, James, 17
Curtiz, Michael, 59, 61, 111, 116

Dade, Frances, 3
Dark Romance: Sexuality in the Horror Film (book), 56
Darrow, Clarence, 35
Darwin, Charles, 33, 103
Daughter of the Dragon, The (1931), 86

Davis, Marjorie Ross, 8
Delehaney, Thornton, 52
Dembow, Sam, 104
Design for Living (1933), 27
Detroit Council of Catholic Organizations, 155
Devil Doll, The (1936), 158
Dinehart, Alan, 136, 138
Doctor X (1932) (film), vii, **55-61**, 109, 111, 114, 117, 119
Doctor X (play), 56
Douglas, Melvyn, 72, 110
Dr. Jekyll and Mr. Hyde (1920) (Paramount film), 2, 18, 21-2
Dr. Jekyll and Mr. Hyde (1931) (film), **19-30**, 42, 56, 97, 129-30, 131, 161
Dr. Jekyll and Mr. Hyde (1941) (film), 20
Dracula (1931) (film), vi, vii, viii, **1-9**, 12, 15, 30, 38, 40, 94, 96, 146, 150, 158
Dracula (1931) (Spanish-language version), 6, 7
Dracula (play), vi, 2, 3, 4, 5
Dracula (novel), vi, 4
Dracula's Daughter (1936), 158

Earles, Daisy, 40, 43
Earles, Harry, 40, 41, 42, 43
Eck, Johnny, 42, 45, 46
Educational Screen, The (periodical), 90
Esper, Dwain, 45
Estes, P.G., 124
Everson, William K., 77, 128, 131, 133

Famous Monsters of Filmland (periodical), 18, 161
Faragoh, Francis Edwards, 13
Farrell, Glenda, vii, 114, 115, 118
Faulkner, William, 28

Film Daily (periodical), 27, 28, 59, 60-1, 105
Fitzgerald, F. Scott, 43
Fleischer, Max, v
Fleming, Victor, 20
Florey, Robert, 12, 13, 32, 34, 35, 36, 37
Ford, Wallace, 41
Fort, Garrett, 12
Foster, Preston, 56, 57
Fox, Sidney, 33
Fox West Coast Theatre, 6
Francis, Arlene, 32, 35, 36, 37, 108, 153
Frankenstein (1931) (film), vi, **11-8**, 35, 38, 40, 52, 69, 77, 94, 95, 111, 115, 146, 157, 158, 161
Frankenstein (novel), vi, 13
Frazer, Robert, 49
Freaks (1932), vi, viii, 7, 22, 38, **39-46**, 51, 57, 86, 87, 89, 102, 128, 142, 157
Freud, Sigmund, 88
Freund, Karl, 5, 7, 37, 95, 97
Front Page, The (play), 56
Frye, Dwight, 5, 13, 110, 126
Fulton, John P., 143

Gemora, Charles, 33
Gilchrist, Mrs, Lloyd C., 145, 146
Goldbeck, Willis, 40
Golden Horrors: An Illustrated Critical Filmography, 1931-1939 (book), 41, 73
Granada theater (Santa Barbra, CA), 16
Grant, Lawrence, 87
Grot, Anton, 111

Hall, Charles D., 73
Hall, Huntz, 38
Hall, Jon, 145
Hall, Mordaunt, 111, 123
Halperin, Edward, 46, 48, 138, 139
Halperin, Victor, 46, 48, 136, 138, 139
Hammer Film Productions, 2, 160
Hamnett, Nina, 151, 152
Harpers (publisher), 72
Harris, Marilyn, 14, 15
Harrison's Reports (periodical), 43, 52, 56, 138
Harron, John, 49
Hatton, Rondo, 45
Hays, Will, v
Hearst, William Randolph, 86, 87
Heath, Percy, 27
Herbert, Holmes, 22
Hersholt, Jean, 90
Hickman, R.W., 132
Hilton, Daisy, 42, 43, 45
Hilton, Violet, 42, 43, 45
Hitchcock. Alfred, 160
Hobart, Rose, 21, 22
Hobbes, Halliwell, 22
Hoffenstein, Samuel, 27
Hogan, David J., 56
Hohl, Arthur, 101
Hollywood Dog Training School, 68
Hollywood Horror Film 1931-1941: Madness in a Social Landscape (book), 56, 137
Hollywood Herald, The (periodical), 95
Hollywood on Parade (film series), 124
Hollywood Reporter, The (periodical), 15, 17, 117, 125, 158
Holmes, Phillips, 25
Hopkins, Miriam, 22, 23, 27
Horror of Dracula (1958), 2
House of Fear, The (1945), 142
House of Frankenstein (1944), 153
Howard, Ed., 87
Humphries, Reynold, 56, 137

Hunchback of Notre Dame, The (1923), 2, 3
Hyams, Lelia, 41, 101, 102, 105

International Photographer, The (periodical), 69
International Pictures, 159
Invincible Pictures Corporation, 157
Invisible Man, The (1933), vii, viii, 140, **141-7**
Invisible Man: A Grotesque Romance, The (novel), 140, 143, 144
Invisible Man Returns, The (1940), 145
Invisible Man's Revenge, The (1944), 145
Island of Dr. Moreau, The (novel), 98, 100, 103, 105, 140
Island of Lost Souls, The (1932), viii, 13, 24, 29, 97, 98, **99-106**, 129, 131, 136, 139, 140, 142, 146, 157
Jacobs, W.W., viii
Janney, William, 76
Jefferis, A.B., 117, 124
Jensen, Paul, 144
Johann, Zita, 94, 96, 97
Johnson, Noble, 36, 66, 96
Johnson, Tom, 18, 23, 49, 96
Jones, Guy, 28
Journey's End (1930), 72
Joy, Jason S., 3, 8, 17, 22, 27, 56, 76, 103
Jump Cut (periodical), 50
Jungle Captive, The (1945), 142

Kane, Eddie, 96
Kansas City *Star* (periodical), 43
Kansas State Board of Censors, 17
Karloff, Boris, vi, 13, 14, 16, 18, 69, 72, 75, 77, 86, 87, 88, 89, 90, 91, 92, 94, 97, 106,

128, 143, 146, 151, 152, 153, 154, 157, 158
Kazanjian, Aram, 37
Kenton, Erle C., 102
King Kong (1933), vii, viii, 33, **121-6**, 161
Kinnell, Murray, 42
Kohner, Paul, 7

Laemmle, Carl, Jr., 3, 7, 15, 16, 17, 35, 72, 76
Laemmle, Carl, Sr., 2, 3, 9, 15, 16, 92
Laemmle, Carla, 7
Lambert, Gavin, 12
Lashley, Dick, 60
Laughton, Charles, vi, 29, 101, 105, 109, 133
Legion of Decency, v, 147, 155
Lewis, Charles E., 38
Lewis, David, 16
Lewis, Herschell Gordon, 160
Lewton, Val, 159
Lindsay, Cynthia, 89
Lloyd, Harold, 68
Lodge, John, 130
Lodger, The (1944), 159
Lombard, Carole, vi, 133, 135, 136, 138
London After Midnight (1927), 2
Lorre, Peter, 157
Los Angeles *Examiner* (periodical), 132
Los Angeles *Record* (periodical), 90
Los Angeles *Times* (periodical), 8, 105, 132
Loveday, Raoul, 151
Loy, Myrna, vi, 87, 89, 91, 133
Lubitsch, Ernst, 27
Lugosi, Bela, vi, 3, 4, 8, 9, 12, 13, 25, 29, 32, 38, 46, 48, 49, 53, 91, 96,

103, 106, 124, 128, 146, 150, 152, 154, 157, 158
Lugosi, Hope Lininger, 4
Luke, Keye, 92
Lund, Lucille, 151
Lusk, Norbert, 68, 132
Lyric Theatre (Greenville, IL), 132

Mad Love (1935), 157
Mad Monster, The (1942), 104
Magic Island, The (book), 48
Majestic Studios, vi, 105, 108
Mamoulian, Rouben, vii, 20, 21, 23, 24, 25, 26, 28, 29, 161
Man Made Monster (1941), 109
Man Who Changed His Mind, The (1936), 158
Mank, Gregory William, 4, 96, 102, 159
Manners, David, 5, 7, 35, 94, 152, 154
March, Fredric, vi, 21, 23, 25, 27, 29
Mark of the Vampire, The (1935), 157
Marshek, Archie, 68
Mask of Fu Manchu, The (1932), vii, 77, **85-92**, 133, 161
Massey, Raymond, 74
Maxwell, Edwin, 114
Mayer, Louis B., 40, 89
Mayfair Theatre (New York City, NY), 37, 38
McCrea, Joel, 65, 68
McHugh, Frank, 114
Meehan, Leo, 17
Melford, George, 6, 7
Melincoff, Max, 60
Mescall, John J., 152
Metro-Goldwyn-Mayer (MGM), vi, 2, 29, 38, 40, 43, 44, 77, 86, 89, 157, 158, 159
Michigan Catholic (periodical), 155
Midland Theatre (Kansas City, MO), 44
Miller, Miriam, 28
Milwaukee *Sentinel* (periodical), 52
Modern Screen (periodical), 68, 90, 95, 124
Moffit, John C., 43, 44
Moncure, R.C.L., 104
Monkey's Paw, The (1933) (film), viii, 161
"Monkey's Paw, The" (story), viii
Monogram Pictures Corporation, 91, 92, 159
Monster Show: A Cultural History of Horror, The (book), 36, 116
Moore, Eva, 73
Morley, Karen, 91
Mosher, John, 44
Most Dangerous Game, The (1932) (film), vii, **63-9**, 119
"Most Dangerous Game, The" (short story), vii, 64, 66, 67
Motion Picture Association of America rating system, 160
Motion Picture Herald (periodical), 17, 28, 38, 60, 68, 76, 96, 108, 117, 124, 131, 139, 146
Motion Picture Magazine (periodical), 4, 128
Motion Pictures Producers and Distributors of America (MPPDA), v, 8, 13, 56
Mummy, The (1932), vi, vii, 92, **93-8**, 161
Mummy's Curse, The (1944), 97
Mummy's Ghost, The (1944), 97
Mummy's Hand, The (1940), 96
Mummy's Tomb, The (1942), 96-7
Murder by the Clock (1931), 25

Murders in the Rue Morgue (1932) (film), vii, 12, **31-8**, 103, 108, 122, 142, 146, 153
"Murders in the Rue Morgue" (story), 29, 32
Murders in the Zoo (1933), vi, 24, 33, 57, 64, 94, 109, 115, 126, **127-33**, 137, 139, 142
Museum of Modern Art, 45
Mussolini, Benito, 151
My Man Godfrey (1936), 135
Mysterious Fu Manchu, The (1929), 86
Mysterious Mr. Wong, The (1935), 91
Mystery of Life, The (1931), 35, 37
Mystery of the Wax Museum (1933), vii, viii, 61, **113-9**, 124, 125, 139, 154, 161

Nagel, Anne, 109
New Movie Magazine (periodical), 60
New Piedmont Theatre (Piedmont, MO), 117, 124
New York *Daily News* (periodical), 117
New York *Herald Tribune* (periodical), 44
New York *Post* (periodical), 52, 117
New York State Board of Censors, 35, 37
New York *Times* (periodical), 27, 38, 76, 89, 117, 123, 132, 152
New Yorker (periodical), 44
Noll, Lonnie, 38
Nollen, Scott Allen, 74
Norton, Edgar, 23
Nothing Sacred (1937), 135

O'Brien, Willis H., 125
"Occulta", 139
O'Connor, Robert Emmett, 119
O'Connor, Una, 143

Odeon Theatre (Chandler, OK), 77
Ohio Department of Film Censorship, The, 116
Old Dark House, The (1932), vii, viii, 69, **71-77**, 161
Oland, Warner, 86
On the Other Hand (book), 126
Only the Cinema (blog), 87
Opera House, The (Foley, MN), 76
Origin of Species, The (book), 33
Osbourne, Vivienne, 137

Palace Theatre (Lawrence, MA), 60
Paramount Pictures, vi, 18, 21, 24, 25, 40, 53, 86, 97, 100, 102, 104, 105, 124, 126, 129, 130, 131, 132, 133, 135, 137, 138
Paramount Theatre (Los Angeles, CA), 132
Parent-Teacher Association (PTA), 8, 145
Pearl of Death, The (1944), 45
Phantom of the Opera (1925), 3
Photoplay (periodical), 28, 44, 117
Picture of Dorian Gray, The (1945), 159
Picture Play Magazine (periodical), 38, 68
Pierce, Jack, 14, 69, 94
Pichel, Irving, 25
Poe, Edgar Allan, 29, 30, 32, 146, 152, 157
Porcasi, Paul, 124
Pre-Code.com (website), 153
Preminger, Otto, 160
Price, Vincent, 145
Priestley, J.B., 72, 73
Private Life of Henry the Eighth, The (1933), 29
Producers Releasing Corporation, 159
Production Code, v, vi, vii, viii, 3, 8, 27, 42, 44, 50, 53, 91, 95, 96, 103,

108, 109, 118, 122, 123, 129, 131, 132, 136, 138, 142, 143, 144, 145, 150, 152, 153, 155, 157, 159, 160
Production Code Administration, 35, 147, 157, 158, 159
Psycho (1960), 160
Pye, Merrill, 43

Rains, Claude, vi, vii, 143, 145
Randian, 42, 45, 46
Rapf, Harry, 43
Rasputin and the Empress, The (1932), 89
Raven, The (1935), 97, 152, 157
Regina Theatre (Los Angeles, CA), 53, 158
Reid, Danny, 153
Republic Pictures, 157
Return of Fu Manchu, The (1930), 86
Rialto (New York, NY), 104
Rivoli Theatre (New York, NY), 28
RKO-Radio Pictures, vi, 61, 69, 119, 123, 125, 126, 145, 159
Roach, Bert, 33
Robbins, Tod, 40, 41
Rohauer, Raymond, 29
Rohmer, Sax, 86, 90
Rose, Ruth, 123
Rosener, George, 57
Rossitto, Angelo, 42
Roxy, The (New York, NY), 5-6, 8
Royal Family, The (1930), 25
Roxy Theater (New York, NY), 145
Ruggles, Charlie, 131, 132, 133

S.O.S. Coast Guard (1937), 158
S.T. Theatre (Parker, SD), 124
San Francisco *Examiner* (periodical), 152
Sanctuary (novel), 28

Scarlet Street (online forum), 161
Scheuer, Philip K., 8, 105
Schlitze, 43
Schoedsack, Ernest, 66, 68
Schulberg, B.P., 22
Scopes, John T., 35
Scott, Randolph, 132, 133, 137
Screen Actors Guild, 21, 97
Screen Play (periodical), 153
Seabrook, William, 48
Secret of the Blue Room, The (1933), 76
Selig Zoo, 68
Senn, Bryan, 41, 73
Sennwald, Andre, 132
Shelley, Mary Wollstonecraft, vi, 13
Sherlock Holmes and the Voice of Terror (1942), 142
Sherriff, R.C., 73, 144, 146
Show, The (1927), 40
Silver, Ben, 68
Silver Family Theatre (Greenville, MI), 68
Silver Screen (periodical), 145, 146
Sin in Soft Focus: Pre-Code Hollywood (book), 24
Skal, David J., 36, 116
Skinner, B.O., 116
Son of Frankenstein (1939), 53, 158
Son of Kong (1933), viii
Sooky (1931), 28
"Spurs" (short story), 40, 41
Standing, Joan, 5
Starrett, Charles, 87, 88
State Theatre (Minneapolis, MN), 44
Steiner, Max, 125
Steinke, Hans, 101
Stettmund, Gerald, 76
Stevens, Landers, 67
Stevenson, Robert Louis, vii, 2, 18, 20, 21, 24, 26
Stitt, Ralph, 28

Stoker, Bram, vi, 4
Stone, Lewis. 90
Stone, Millburn, 104
Story of Temple Drake, The (1933), 28
Strand Theatre (Louisville, KY), 3
Strange, Glenn, 104
Strange Case of Dr. Jekyll and Mr. Hyde, The (novella), 2, 18, 20, 21, 24
Strayer, Frank, 108
Stroheim, Erich von, 126
Struss, Karl, 27
Stuart, Gloria, 73, 75, 76, 77, 143
Stubbs, Harry, 142
Supernatural (1933), 22, **135-40**
Sutherland, Edward, 127, 129
Sutton, John, 145
Svengali (1931), 49

Terror Aboard (1933), 131
Thalberg, Irving, 40
Thesiger, Ernest, 72
Time (periodical), 52, 152
Tovar, Lupita, 6
Tracy, Lee, vii, 56
Tracy, Spencer, 20, 29
Trotti, Lamar, 56
Trouble in Paradise (1932), 27
Turner, George E., 53
Twentieth Century (1934), 136
Twentieth Century Fox, 86, 159

Ulmer, Edgar G., 37, 150, 151, 153
Umann, E. Mark, 158
United Artists, vi
United Artists theater (San Francisco, CA), 52
Universal Horrors: The Studio's Classic Films, 1931-1946 (book), 8, 34, 72, 73
Universal-International Pictures, 159

Universal Pictures, v, vi, 2, 3, 5, 6, 7, 9, 12, 16, 17, 18, 29, 32, 34, 35, 36, 38, 40, 45, 53, 69, 73, 76, 77, 92. 96, 97, 140, 142, 144, 145, 146, 150, 152, 157, 158, 159
Unknown, The (1927), 6, 40
Unholy Three, The (1925), 40, 42
Unholy Three, The (1930), 42

Vampire Bat, The (1933), 105, **107-11**, 126
Van Sloan, Edward, 5, 16, 17, 18, 94
Variety (periodical), 8, 29, 38, 52, 64, 90, 91, 95, 104, 105, 109, 139
Venice Film Festival, 45
Very Witching Time of Night: Dark Alleys of Classic Horror Cinema, The (book), 102
Victor, Henry, 41
Victoria, Queen of the United Kingdom of Great Britain and Ireland, 21
Vidor, Charles, 89
Vieira, Mark A., 24
Virtue (1932), 136

Walking Dead, The (1936), 158
Warner, H.B., 137
Warner, Jack, 56, 117
Warner Brothers, vi, 53, 57, 59, 61, 111, 114, 115, 116, 117, 119, 158
Warner Theater (Milwaukee, WI), 52
Warner theater (Pittsburgh, PA), 52
Washington Post (periodical), 95
Waterloo Bridge (1931), 72
Watts, Richard, Jr., 44
Weaver, Tom, 8, 21, 34, 72
Webb, Kenneth, 48
Wedding March, The (1928), 126
Welles, Orson, 86

Wells, H.G, vii, 98, 100, 101, 103, 105, 140, 144, 146
Wells, Jacqueline (later Julie Bishop), 152
Werewolf of London (1935), 157
West of Zanzibar (1928), 7
Westmore, Perc, 115
Whale, James, vii, 12, 13, 14, 15, 16, 17, 18, 24, 69, 72, 73, 75, 76, 77, 140, 144, 146, 157
What's My Line? (television program), 32
White Woman (1933), 136
White Zombie (1932), vii, **47-53**, 96, 102, 136
Wilder, Billy, 160
Wilkerson, W.R., 15, 17
Williams, Tony, 50
Wills, Brember, 73
Wilson (1944), 110
Winter, Mrs. Thomas G., 139
Wolf Man, The (1941), 159
Wolfe, Ian, 97
Women in Horror Films, 1930s (book), 101
Wray, Fay, vi, vii, 53, 57, 61, 64, 65, 109, 111, 115, 116, 118, 119, 122, 124, 125, 126
Wray, John, 57, 58
Wylie, Philip, 100

Young, Waldemar, 100
Young Man, The (periodical), 100

Zanuck, Darryl F., 110
Zombie (play), 48
Zucco, George, 104
Zukor, Adolph, 25

Also available from BearManor Media

**Another Nice Mess:
The Laurel & Hardy Story**
RAYMOND VALINOTI, JR.
Laurel & Hardy biography for kids.
ISBN 9781593935467
$14.95

www.ingramcontent.com/pod-product-compliance
Lightning Source LLC
Chambersburg PA
CBHW051930160426
43198CB00012B/2097